WHERE EAGLES SOAR

WILLIAM EARLE CAMERON

Where Eagles Soar

WILLIAM EARLE CAMERON

Cross Cultural Publications, Inc.

CrossRoads Books

Also by William Earle Cameron:

GREAT DRAMAS OF THE BIBLE

Biblical quotations used in this book are from The Authorized King James Version, unless otherwise noted.

Published by **CROSS CULTURAL PUBLICATIONS, INC.**
CROSS ROADS BOOKS
Post Office Box 506
Notre Dame, Indiana, 46556, U.S.A.
Phone: (219) 272-0889
FAX: (219) 273-5973

ISBN: 0-940121-16-6
Library of Congress Catalog Card Number: 94-71044

Dedication

To

those

on the threshold...

A

Spiritual

Alternative

To

Negative Religion

Acknowledgment

To my beloved daughter Heather, the best reason God has gifted me in my life for dedicating it to the Angels' Promise - the dawning age of The Wonderful Child that can be the anointed future for all humankind - ''Glory to God in the highest, and on earth peace, good will toward men'' (Luke 2:14)

Contents

Introduction

These days a great many individuals are aware of something vital missing in their lives. They also see a similar void in the life of the society around them. During more than a quarter of a century of spiritual counseling to a large cross section of people, this deep feeling among the people has become increasingly apparent to me. They yearn for something more, something higher, something of a greater reality from which to reorient and truly fulfill their lives. Indeed, a remarkable spiritual awakening is taking place around us. The amazing thing is that it is not just the churchgoing people who are entering the threshold of spiritual awaking, but even the unchurched and agnostics. This powerful positive force is, however, countered by a negative force. Sadly enough, this comes from the well meaning church community who turn away those who seek solace and enlightenment with their negative interpretations of what the Bible and Christian values are all about. With all the dogmatic religious claims that abound, people often do not know where to turn.

A landmark experience in my own life made me come to grips with this dilemma in a spiritually compelling way. It occurred during my second entry into civilian life from the military. I was facing a ''Best Years Of Our Lives'' syndrome of difficult adjustment not untypical of many war veterans. Admittedly a fairly drastic case, I had lost any sense of real meaning or purpose to life; and, as a disillusioned and somewhat bitter young man, had come to regard the brotherhood of man as a grim joke.

Then came an unforeseen spiritual intervention. The sudden and exalted regeneration, which included a healing as well as a new vision of life - accompanied by an awakening to the spiritual reality behind it - all seemed quite miraculous to me. And, like the Apostle Paul after his soul-shaking Damascus Road experience, I found that all of this just could not be contained in the old religious model. Much of conventional churchology had become ''cotton candy.''

For one thing, I was no longer susceptible to being frightened into salvation, or compromised into a sectarian characterization of worthiness. At first startled and then dismayed by the negative undercurrent of hard-shelled proselytization, I began to see through so much of the adversarial strategy of this fear-based approach. More than anything else, in the glow of the fresh hope and promise of my newly born life, I truly wanted to become a part of something that was affirmatively ''for'' the good and Godly; not bellicosely ''against'' a continuously perceived epidemic of the bad. My quest, therefore, began with a search for an authentic spiritual life in which I could truly give myself to furthering the integration and spiritual unification of humankind into a real brotherhood; not in inadvertently perpetuating the abysmal ''slash and burn'' alienations of religiosity.

In the years that followed, I dedicated myself to an intensive study of the Bible and Its related historical and religious background, drawing on the research and commentary of the available wealth of Judeo-Christian scholarship. I understood the reasons, which were pragmatic, for which the early Church imposed rigidity in dogma. I also understood how liturgy and ecclesiastical structure became ossified in the Middle Ages. Furthermore, I realized how difficult it is for institutions and individuals, entrenched in a pattern of existence, to make a change, except through a regeneration.

But, again as with Paul, the ''Light'' involving my personal spiritual awakening centered around Jesus. Accordingly, it is the actual life and the original teachings of Jesus that have become the central and final authority for His Spiritual Truth in my life. More and more, I have learned to make an important distinction between ''religious'' and ''spiritual.''

The miraculous spiritual awakening I experienced was not an isolated incident. There is a wave of spiritual regeneration sweeping the entire world. This powerful tide is breaking down walls, empires and institutions of the past; and, with a cumulative ascendancy, creating new possibilities for a higher life of everyone on the planet (often woefully resisted by those still entrenched in old systems and models). People of all nations, cultures and religions are energized and elevated into a higher spirituality. There is also a ground swell recognition that behind this collective transcendence is an inspired and spiritually empowered force for good.

So to those who must now seek outside the pale of orthodox religion for spirituality, might also be added the numerous people within Christianity who have accepted Jesus, but not yet His spiritual principles - especially for truly living the Larger Life ("I am come that they might have life, and that they might have it more abundantly" John 10:10).

After centuries of superimposed religious doctrine and dogma, it is not without merit to consider that Jesus might actually be one of the most misunderstood personages in Christianity. Yet the entirety of truth, ideals and principles which underlie all life await our recognition and acceptance right within His Own teachings and example. This book is a biblically-based journey of rediscovery into Jesus' approach to life. It converges on how we can make a turn-around, enter the spiritual path and begin a real life of becoming what we were created to be - according to Jesus.

As a prelude, the first turnabout is a revealing look at how He, Himself, regarded and promoted our defamed potential. We have focused on saying that Jesus was God. He put it another way. He said very pointedly that it was God in Him Who was God ("...the words I speak unto you I speak not of myself: but the Father that dwelleth in me, he doeth the works" John 14:10). And then He formulated His message around revealing to us the long concealed Spiritual Truth that the very same God indwells each of us. He focused on **us** - Wake up! Come to yourselves! You have a precious and privileged Divine Heritage awaiting right within you!

We have felt that we revere Jesus best by regarding Him as the Great Exception. He would have us honor Him - and follow Him - as the Great Example, the Divine Wayshower to our own spiritual fulfillment. His mission was to disclose to all humanity "The mystery hid for ages...which is **Christ in you**, the hope of glory" (Colossians 1:26,27). We have thought that we are saved only through lowering and diminishing our basic nature to that of "born sinner." He would have us regard ourselves as God's children in the process of "growing up" ("Unto the measure of the stature of the fullness of Christ" Ephesians 4:13) and revere our Essential Nature as spiritual. He presented us with the Spiritual Truth that He said would "Set us free" and lead us out of all our fledgling human mistakes and upward into our spiritual maturity.

Jesus gave us the correctives that enable us to make the pivotal Prodigal turn, through the redeeming of our mistaken identity. He admonished, "Ye know not what manner of spirit ye are of" (Luke 9:55). Then, through His own Christhood, He revealed "The way, and the truth and the life" in which we discover and unfold our latent God-given potential toward the ultimate spiritual fulfillment of every human being destined from the beginning as "God's Image."

Jesus also heightened to its supreme glory the "Good News" of our divine birthright as heirs of God by revealing exactly just "What manner of spirit" constitutes our spiritual legacy - from a God of love. With allegorical emphasis, Jesus accented the extent of God's all-embracing love to include the loving care of "The sparrow in the field." Then, in His "Sermon On The Mount," He categorically contrasted the amplitude between God's nurturing regard for even "The fowls of the air" with that for every single human being: "Are ye not much better than they" (Matthew 6:26). With this, Jesus would have us realize that the sparrow is important to God, but not a likely model for a human life. In His day, sparrows infested Palestine. They were noisy and troublesome, and figurative symbols for anything ordinary, commonplace and of little value. They lived small, earth-bound, tremulous lives, aspiring to nothing beyond grubbing for food and mundane comfort. The Hebrew word for sparrow meant "to chirp or twitter." There is an old adage that when the sparrow says "peep," it thinks it has said everything there is to say.

Paramount to truly comprehending the Gospel is the Bible's highest declaration of our Creator's love: "God so loved the world that he gave his only begotten Son that whosoever believeth on him, should not perish, but have eternal life" (John 3:16).

God's "Only begotten" is God's Parent Spirit Nature, the complete, perfect and only Nature God has. Most have not grasped the essence of Jesus' Good News that the bestowal of this spiritual Image and Likeness was the First Birth of every Child of God. Most, therefore, have not yet discerned the core Spiritual Truth of our being - manifest through the Life of Jesus,

"The Logos (Creative Principle) made flesh" - that God created each of us in the Seed-Likeness of the Divine Image. Then relating the creative process of "everything he had made" to the development and fruition of that Spiritual Resemblance (Sonship), God beheld us, both essentially and potentially, "Very good" (Genesis 1:31).

Nor have most religions redeemed their own negative view of humanity enough to concede that the original inherent spiritual perfection of the Genesis pronouncement for God's children has never been flawed - a mutually exclusive impossibility. In addition, neither has it ever been withdrawn, or vilified to "innately sinful" - a tangential presumption totally counter to the essential character and integrity of God. Instead, the truth about our essential Spiritual Nature has doggedly been misunderstood, disregarded, spurned and obscured. Most have not yet dared to recognize that Jesus' true mission was to bear witness not only to His Divinity, but ours, "The true Light, which lighteth every man that cometh into the world" (John 1:9).

Very few, therefore, have fully accepted Jesus as both a Personal Savior and an ever-present Divine Exemplification and intimate Spiritual Benefactor to inspire and guide each of us constantly in becoming, by divine design, what God created us to be - Christed Beings. Yet, this was directly suggested throughout His Teaching. None of the highlight on our own intrinsic "joint-heir" possibilities (Romans 8:17) takes anything away from the Christhood of Jesus: "Son of God" and "Son of man." It does unveil the hidden divine potential in all of us that He came to reveal and greatly increases the power and scope of Jesus' transformational message to each of us.

Perhaps the best place to launch ourselves into the abiding possibilities of Jesus' life from the Inner Spirit is to simply accept, as a corollary birthright, our inalienable **prerogative** of **higher consciousness**. Then, through the inspiration and guidance of the Beautiful Attitudes in His Sermon On The Mount, allow this to be the ascending path by which we are lifted into a higher state of identity as children of God and all that awaits that divine estate.

The eagle is a fitting emblem for those who have awakened to the truth of their inborn spiritual identity ("Born again") and aspire to truly follow Jesus in the divinely intended fulfillment of their evolving Christhood. The eagle is a magnificent bird, powerful and swift and destined for high flight. To the ancient Hebrews, "The way of an eagle in the air" (Proverbs 30:19) was considered one of the great wonders of life. The eagle is constituted to withstand any storm and rise above any earthly bondage. Challenge and hardship only serve to discipline and strengthen it. The power and range of its vision are extraordinary. The eagle is reputedly the only creature on earth that can look unblinkingly into the sun; and glancing into the periphery, it can still sharply discern everything around and beneath its vantage point. It, therefore, achieves the high vision and represents the glory that can be attained only from life's loftiest point of view. The spirit of the eagle will never be satisfied to remain half-alive on the ground.

Those with the faith and spiritual audacity to aspire for the heights of Jesus' most challenging promise "He that believeth on me, the works that I do shall he do also, and greater works than these shall he do" (John 14:12) shall, indeed, "Mount up with wings as eagles" (Isaiah 40:31) and live their lives with "The look of the eagle in their eye."

Chapter One

The View From the Mount

The Christ of the Sermon On The Mount is different from the Christ of the creeds. This small but important part of the Bible (contained within Matthew, chapters 5 - 7 and Luke, chapter 6:2O - 49) comprises one of the greatest documents ever compiled. Yet, while much of the world pays homage to it, even many Christians do not clearly understand Jesus' Sermon on the Mount from the spiritual point of view.

From a spiritual perspective, the Sermon on the Mount provides a revolutionary strategy and guide for consciousness expansion and spiritual development. It also serves as a divine blueprint for entering and experiencing life as the creative opportunity and spiritual adventure that God intended. But in spite of the many positive biblical promises of our Children of God endowments and birthright, the negative theological view of ourselves has perpetuated a strange blindness to our true identity. Major religions regard humanity as "fallen," "unsaved" and "unworthy." This debasement has drastically curtailed the awareness of our spiritual possibilities. The splendor of our potential, the transcendent dimensions of our minds and hearts and our latent capacity for spiritual achievement are indeed revolutionary ideas to most people.

Formalized religion has tended to relegate the actual teachings of Jesus to an insignificant role in its dispensation of doctrinal instructions that have evolved around eschatology - a theological term for "the end of the world" - borrowed originally from the Zoroastrian religion of ancient Persia. This perpetuates the belief and mandates our enlistment in an imminent, climactic fight between good and evil (which, right in the midst of the Sermon On The Mount, Jesus explicitly admonished us against: "But I say unto you, That ye resist not evil" Matthew 5:39).

This concept also placed grave emphasis on a God of wrath and doom and a thoroughly disparaging view of humanity as hopelessly flawed, helpless and, by the time of Augustine, branded with the essential identity of "sinner." In this grim, negative perspective, the Sermon On The Mount is considered merely an "interim ethic": A way of behaving yourself and holding on while awaiting rescue and evacuation; provided, of course, that you are a member in good standing of the proper ecclesiastical institution. But none of this is contained in the spiritual teachings of Jesus.

There is also the problem of translation. The Bible as we know it today is several times removed from the Aramaic language in which Jesus originally spoke. Its colorful, idiomatic characteristics and especially the treasury of Eastern spiritual symbology that permeates the Bible are usually lost on Western minds and missed by the translators and interpreters.

These problems often cause the Beatitudes from the Sermon on the Mount to appear as either weapons of restraint against our "original sinful nature" or as an ambivalent system of standards seemingly "upside down" to all we have learned to really value and aim for in our lives. And - even though some of the implied morality constrictions might fit their viewpoint - in some seminaries that focus on the negative, anyone showing too much interest in the spiritual significance of the Sermon On The Mount is highly suspect.

The True Gospel

The most overlooked aspect in Christianity is the true magnitude of Jesus' Gospel. His message is really "Good News"! He revealed a God of infinite love: an all-good, completely benevolent, totally loving Spiritual Parent of all humanity. Correspondingly, He disclosed the glorious tidings of our own true spiritual nature as eternal Children of God and established the truth about our divine heritage of the often hidden but vast inner reservoirs of spiritual potential that God vested in us when He created us "In his own image" (Genesis 1:27).

In rather forthright symbology, when Jesus said "Ye are the light of the world" (Matthew 5:14), He was linking our essential spiritual nature with His ("I am the light of the world" John 8:12). He was also proclaiming to each of us that, by the design principle of our being (Christ) we too are divinely designated by God as causative, radiant centers for expressing the same creative essence that runs the universe. Likewise, when He gave us the startling summons, "Be ye therefore perfect, even as your Father which is in heaven is perfect" (Matthew 5:48), He was disclosing to all of us the destined possibilities of manifesting, through the universal creative process working within us, the same pattern of perfection in our own lives that we witness in Him as the "Word made flesh" (John 1:14).

It was in the enlightened revelation of the Apostle Paul in his letter to the Colossians that we are given - outright - the crowning recognition of the Christ of God as the spiritually Higher Self concealed in the Image of the Divine inherent in every person: "Even the mystery which hath been hid from ages...which is CHRIST IN YOU, the hope of glory: whom we proclaim, admonishing every man, and teaching every man in all wisdom; that we may present every man PERFECT IN CHRIST" (Colossians 1:26-28 ASV). Paul, through spiritual discernment, understood the true estate of humanity. He stated clearly that the ultimate mystery of spiritual truth unveiled in Jesus' life concerned the presence of a latent Christ in all: "The Spirit itself beareth witness with our spirit, that we are the children of God: And if children, then heirs; heirs of God, and joint heirs with Christ" (Romans 8:16,17).

Jesus, all through His ministry, taught and demonstrated that we are here to discover and express the inherent nature of God in us. The "Good News" is that the Divine lives in us! ("Know ye not that ye are the temple of God, and that the Spirit of God dwelleth in you?" I Corinthians 3:16). It proclaims, over and over, what God's Spirit indwelling us can do through us: That we can change and grow, overcome and transcend all our generic misconceptions and humanly endowed limitations. Above all, we can bring forth the latent qualities of Christ (God-in-us) into our consciousness and increasingly give creative self-expression in our human lives to the inherent spiritual nature of God within ("Verily, verily, I say unto you, He that believeth on me (Christ), the works that I do shall he do also; and greater works than these shall he do; because I go unto my Father" John 14:12).

From Jesus' point of view, we are all candidates for

Christ Consciousness. He often emphasized that the great secret and supreme mark in life ("The pearl of great price," "The treasure hid in a field") was in giving prime consideration to the inner realm of spiritual resources, potentials and qualities found in Higher Consciousness ("Seek ye first the Kingdom of God" Matthew 6:33 - "Neither shall they say, Lo here! or, lo there!, for, behold the kingdom of God is within you" Luke 17:21).

The Christ Principle

The Sermon On The Mount discloses the principles and attitudes we can use in our inward, spiritual development. It is actually a portrait of Jesus Himself: The ultimate revelation of the great Christ Principle - the eternal spiritual identity of a Child of God ("A pattern unto them which should hereafter believe on him to life everlasting" I Timothy 1:16). This, the divine nature of Christ expressible in a human life, is the spiritual frame of reference in which to interpret everything Jesus taught. The Beatitudes ("The Beautiful Attitudes") pertain to states of consciousness that first provide the foundation for Christ-like character and then produce the necessary soul growth and spiritual development. They encourage and challenge us ever higher towards Christhood ("The mark for the prize of the high calling of God in Christ Jesus" Philippians 3:14). The Beatitudes can be seen as the spiritual "Flight Plan" for the Upward Way of the disciple of the Christ life.

Divine Happiness

With the repeated use of the word "Blessed," Jesus established with certainty the positive character of the qualitative changes portrayed in and promised by the Beatitudes. Blessed meant "divine happiness": happiness to the "Nth degree," "following our bliss," the "happy ending" in children's stories, the truly "good life." Divinely happy are those who are right within, who realize their true Divine Identity and activate and radiate their spiritual potential. Truly happy are those whose supreme priority is soul growth and whose ruling aspirations are for life as it was meant to be - loving, giving and unfolding their spiritual nature from within. Real happiness always results from looking within to our True Nature and assimilating Its character into our minds and hearts and then our lives.

If on the surface the Beatitudes appear to be a paradox, seemingly contrary to the common sense of a worldly point of view, the word "Spiritual" converts the entire Sermon On The Mount into a "Divine Constitution." It supports our rights and duties as spiritual beings who are endowed with the God-given capacity for spiritual achievement. The word "Spirit" is the key that unlocks all the Good of God that awaits unfoldment through each. Everything Jesus taught concerned Spiritual Truth. What He truly divulged throughout His life and teachings can only be apprehended in that light.

Jesus came primarily to show us how to awaken to our Spiritual Nature and then live our lives on a spiritual basis - as He did. He illustrated in many ways the marvelous possibilities of the Spirit in us. Yet, He said that notwithstanding our tremendous inner potential, we are rarely capable of expressing our latent God-given endowments beyond an equivalent of those qualities and activities being first established in our minds and hearts. We must earn the right of the manifest sovereignty of each new level of our growth and unfoldment by a corresponding increase in consciousness.

Our Evolving Self

Paul characterized our aptitude for unfolding and manifesting our divine heritage in terms of two distinct identity natures: The "Natural man" and the "Spiritual man" ("But the natural man receiveth not the things of the Spirit of God: for they are foolishness unto him: neither can he know them, because they are spiritually discerned" I Corinthians 2:14). Paul was certain that we are destined to evolve higher ("And as we have borne the image of the earthly, we shall also bear the image of the heavenly" I Corinthians 15:49).

Paul's classification of these two modes of existence readily apply to two distinct levels of consciousness. Life based on the intellectual-emotional limits of the "Natural man" consciousness produces all the bondage and ills that we suffer in the human condition. We are admonished by Paul to "Let this mind be in you which was also in Christ Jesus" (Philippians 2:5). Life is consciousness. When God created us "In His **Image** and after His **Likeness**'' - and with the possibilities of expressing His very own (**"Only Begotten"**) Nature in all sorts of wonderful ways - it was also necessary to give us free choice and never directly interfere with that inestimable gift. Yet, as with any loving parent (Jesus' favorite characterization of God), God withholds from the "Natural man" (our personality, human-ego identity) anything of the creative qualities and powers intended for the expression only through our Higher Nature (the "Spiritual man") - lest they be misused. And just as we would never entrust the family car to a small child, our Heavenly Father provides for us the same parental, spiritual safeguards ("And lead us not into temptation, but deliver us from evil" Matthew 6:13).

Jesus made it clear that we are responsible for providing the day by day consciousness through which we experience life. We alone are responsible for keeping our thoughts right and for cultivating the affirmative, ennobling and Truth-oriented attitudes that open us to the transforming influences of Spirit and evolve us into higher orders in the Creative Process.

The Current Imperative

In Jesus' "View From The Mount," He extends to us the long-sought, ascendant vision of our possibilities for spiritual transformation, both as individuals and as a society, and of the imminent evolution of the human race into a new state of higher, spiritually endowed consciousness.

I wonder what history might have been like if our church creeds and doctrines had said, "We believe in the transforming spiritual principles, laws and possibilities revealed by Jesus in the Sermon On The Mount." Even more important is what is now wondrously possible if we accept the true discipleship of "The way, the truth and the life" (John 14:6) of unfolding our own Divinity - and allow Jesus' vision to lift us to the mountain-top perception of what is truly possible for a spiritual you and me in a rapidly changing world.

Yet the Winds of History are even now revolutionizing the entire planet with an evolutionary winged upliftment into new understanding. For this reason the old understanding of the systems, doctrines, dogmas and creeds of the past is now obsolete. The clashes between the customs and thoughts of the past and those emerging today are more than differences of opinion. They are differences created by humanity's ongoing evolution, which is lifting all of us into higher levels of life. It is imperative that we as individuals and as a collective global family link our lives to the spiritual plan and power involved in this evolutionary change. This is what the Christ of the Sermon on the Mount can reveal to those who are open and receptive to Its spiritual meaning.

Chapter Two

Too Poor to Paint - Too Proud to Whitewash

The remarkably uncomplicated proclamation at the heart of Jesus' Gospel is the wonderful promise that a human being can change: Anyone at anytime can be transformed by opening to the Spirit that dwells within their own being. Indeed, most of the symbols and stories in the Bible relate to the spiritual transformation and growth of the individual. Much of the riddle and the drama of our life concerns the continuing struggle within us between two strong forces. One is the inborn, divine urge toward new and higher expressions of our inherent Spiritual Nature. The other is the tenaciously stubborn resistance of our human nature against any change that isn't tightly controlled by the defensive posture of the cumbersome and highly reactionary intellectual-emotional ego-structure. Therein lies part of the true mystery of life on earth.

In this curious enigma involved in our human identity, we often obstruct the channel of our own higher good. Part of us deeply yearns to follow the inner ''call'' to fuller life while the other part desperately clings to the old and holds back. As a result, a major component of our total nature is blocked out - unheeded and unfulfilled - and we remain asleep to a vital and integral aspect of ourselves. We are not ''whole.''

The indispensable need is, in the words of John the Baptist, to ''Repent''; literally to rethink - a radical change of mind and an entirely new perspective. Around this inward experience pivots the all-important awakening and rebirth to the much greater reality of the life of Spirit.

Jesus portrayed the entire drama of ''the great turn-around'' in His classic parable of the Prodigal Son: ''For this my son was dead, and is alive again; he was lost and he is found'' (Luke 15:24). We are, then, aimed by Paul squarely at the ultimate answer to the human dilemma: ''Awake thou that sleepest, and arise from the dead, and Christ shall give thee light'' (Ephesians 5:14).

In His first Beatitude, ''Blessed are the poor in spirit: for theirs is the kingdom of heaven'' (Matthew 5:3), Jesus illumined the entranceway to the level of life He came to reveal: the domain of Spirit. Here, He helps us prepare for change and get started on the enlightened path to the ''Father's house'' (our true ''Home'' - a consciousness of God). He incorporates all the essentials for a spiritual new start: Disarming our fear-based defenses, surmounting false pride and letting go of artificial loyalties and surrendering the negative, and leaving behind all that separates us from God in our belief systems. This first Beatitude is designed to break the barriers of all the resistance and restraints that hold us back and make us receptive to approaching life anew from a spiritual viewpoint.

The exhortation of this gateway Beatitude is timeless: Be open and receptive! Learn something new! Get started! Right where you are! Now!

The Crucial Change

Today, there is yet another compelling incentive for each of us to embrace the promise of this Beatitude, enter through self-change into the transformational process and resolutely begin our destined ascent on the path upward from the humanly egocentric to the spiritually transcendent. Tremendous changes are already underway! The world is in an epic phase of transition and humanity is now entering another era. The world has long awaited this change. Much of the Bible, and, especially the message of Jesus, focused on the prophesied glory of this quantum leap in world transformation, often mistakenly inter- preted in a negative doomsday mode.

Perhaps the first evidence can now be recognized in the American and then the French Revolution; together a giant step in the spiritual emancipation of the individual by the refutation of the Church-propagated ''Divine right of kings'': the separa- tion of church and state. These radical overthrows of Old Guard entrenchment inaugurated a mounting progression of astound- ing changes. With the Industrial Revolution the reformation became all-pervading. Linked with the rise of the scientific method of thought, incredible advances have been made in the phenomenal world. The amazing achievements in communication, medicine, transportation, including space travel, as well as undreamed of luxuries and conveniences brought forth through the development of technology would have been deemed as nothing short of "Miracles" to people of Jesus' times. The real revolution, however, has been in consciousness. Since the turn of the century, our human knowledge has doubled every six to seven years. Information gained from "$E=MC^2$" changed our entire view of the universe.

Yet like the lift-off of a space vehicle, the transition has only been in the first stage. It has been almost exclusively matter and means oriented. One of the "hidden blessings" in life is that extracting profit for "bottom-line" material gain, self-indulgence and its "galloping consumption" eventually has its own built-in inducement for further stages of development - especially in consciousness. Materialism has not solved our problems. Instead it has caused new and precarious predicaments, leaving a strange void of goal confusion, dissatisfaction and misgiving. Following the global conflict of the early 20th Century and the numbness of the 50's, this began to surface in the upheavals of the 60's with the soul-searing issues of Viet Nam. Then followed a characteristically human pendulum-swing extreme in the 80's and 90's of both blind denial, with an intensified pursuit of unequivocally self-serving and self-gratifying ("Yuppie") life-styles, and a heartening and increasingly urgent dedication of many awakening people worldwide to heal the planet and to work and pray for peace on earth.

The struggle between the two divergent attitudes about the backlash and chaos of the extended human and environmental ill-treatment have brought to the forefront the stark realization that none of these mundane endeavors and technical triumphs, as fascinating as they have sometimes been, bring fulfillment to the authentic desires and aspirations of the soul. The ongoing desecration and defilement of our natural and human resources is rapidly leading humanity into tragic self-alienation and even annihilation. The entire global situation and the survival of the planet has now emerged into crisis proportion.

But polarization and crisis are two important tools that God seems to use for transformation. The Chinese recognize this in their character for the word crisis, which contains the symbols for both danger and opportunity. Synthesis, creative whole-making, always results from the resolution of opposites, "thesis" and "antithesis." In the process, the lesser (the "inferior mind") dissolves through transmutation into the higher (the "superior mind") - an important and appealing aspect of the Good News. As human consciousness mounts towards a transformational break-through of a critical mass of spiritually awakening people, perhaps a turning-point will be the humble awareness that our only sin has been selfishness. From this we would learn that our only fear is our long-held belief that we are spiritually separated from God, in Whom we actually "live, and move and have our being...For we are also his offspring" (Acts 17:28) - eternally.

The next stage of transformation, now underway, is the revolutionary spiritualization of human consciousness. We will be transformed by the freeing of our minds into higher levels of inspiration, which then allows our minds to be used for something beyond our present limits ("And Ye shall know the truth, and the truth shall make you free" John 8:32).

There is, therefore, a relevance about Jesus' first Beatitude that is unique and crucial. We are on the threshold of the greatest human adventure ever known. The new frontier is now in inner space, not outer. There is already a growing recognition that the only solutions remaining for the awesome predicaments of humanity are to be found in the most undervalued of all God-gifted beneficial resources: Human potential itself, which awaits largely undiscovered and untapped in the vast reaches of higher, creative consciousness.

The Golden Age

The next level of human development is the spiritual. Like the dawn of a new era, human consciousness is awakening to the Divine and humanity is moving out of the restraints of dogma into the openness of enlightenment. This lends itself as a positive alternative to the doom perception of the "end of the world," which was originally translated as "the end of the age." In this understanding, it means the end of the old world of our strictly human-consciousness and the beginning of a new, transcendent world of living in Christ Consciousness.

In a conversation with Nicodemus, a Pharisee, Jesus began to define this universally possible, yet intensely personal, transformation into higher, spiritualized consciousness as being "Born again." As with the parable of the Prodigal Son, it pivots around the redeeming ego-identity shift in which we "Come to ourselves," take up the divine birthright of our spiritual identification and begin to come into our true heritage as an Offspring of God.

The era we are now entering holds incredible blessings of peace, love, and creativity. It is truly a Spiritual Renaissance. Most of us have felt the tremors of change in the world and the world needs to change. All world change for the better will come about through the discovery and release of the hidden gifts and spiritual possibilities of transformed individuals.

Few people are aware that they posses within themselves the greatest powers at our disposal to transcend their present human-ego selves by being spiritually born into a greater self; and, in the process, help take humanity into another higher world. To change history, we need only to change ourselves. We change through the expansion and spiritualization of our consciousness. We can now begin to see how important the first Beatitude is in getting our individual selves ready by preparing to lay aside the superficial constraints of the present belief systems and move onto the "mount" of a new state of consciousness and a new level of life.

While in the Marine Corps, I had a buddy named Murphy (somewhat of a "professional Irishman") who once described his family to me as, "too poor to paint - too proud to whitewash." This seems to graphically describe the dilemma of the family of humanity. The majority of people don't really live. Their debilitating predicament is that they don't know this - and, ironically, they don't want to know it. They are deadlocked between ignorance, especially the dire poverty of spiritual awareness, and a false pride in all the illusions that have been conjured through what Paul called the "glass darkly" of human-ego perceptions.

Human consciousness tends to become trapped in its own concepts. One of the most consistent and saddest traits in human history is the difficulty a new idea has in being accepted by the prevailing mind-set.

Foremost in the opportunities available in this life is the utilization of every single experience as a way to learn and grow. Earth-life is a wondrous school. We can learn something important from every person we meet and every circumstance we encounter. One of the most regrettable testimonies possible for a human life is that it was lived uncorrected by experience. Yet, many people die in old age with the same toxic beliefs and prejudices they learned as children.

Poor in Spirit

In the first Beatitude, the initiatory step into the blessed life of spiritually-based living, Jesus tells us how to get off dead-center, make the turnabout homeward to the Father and join the Family Business. The original meaning of the word heaven was "expansion." The promised "Kingdom of Heaven" literally refers to the expanding dimensions of living that are accessible only from the potential of Spirit that can be generated from within ourselves - the activity of the Holy Spirit - the highest possible way to live! Nothing should be more welcome to our ears.

Yet, "Poor in Spirit" are strange words to Western ears. It is true that the word "poor" in the financial sense was adopted by the early church as a virtue of this world in deferment for later rewards in "afterlife." But Jesus never advocated worldly poverty. Rather, He taught and proved God's ever present abundance, starting with inner wealth and its right use. ("It is your Father's good pleasure to give you the Kingdom" Luke 12:32 - "But seek ye first the kingdom of God, and his righteousness, and all these things shall be added unto you" Matthew 6:33.)

Nor did Jesus mean "poor-spirited": self-depreciation, self-disdain and self-invalidation. It is important for humanity to accept and cherish the spiritual realization that we are NOT essentially "sinners"; but we are eternally Children of God! What Jesus did mean was humility in its proper sense, which is neither humiliation, nor pious self-effacement.

True humility is the result of an honest and accurate

appraisal of oneself. We get ourselves into a proper perspe-
tive about our true place in the universe. The one thing we
usually leave out is the spiritual investment that God made in
each of us when He created us "In his own image" (Genesis
1:27) and endowed us with our abiding spiritual inheritance -
and all that it represents. Rarely would anyone, for example, in
attempting to prepare even the most convincingly favorable job
resume, venture to record the enormous assets of their spiritual
birthright as a "Child of God." We would be even more
reluctant to mention that we are a Christ "in the making." Yet,
a truly accurate estimate of ourselves must pay heed to the
divine endowments of our inner selves and acknowledge our
inherent faculty to live from the Christ Principle.

True humility recognizes that in our human identity we
are not complete. At the same time it also gives the Spiritual
Nature of God's potential in us a rightful place in the development and fulfillment of our lives. True humility adheres to being
true to the possibilities of our True Self. One of Jesus' superb
examples was of Himself: "The Father that dwelleth in me, he
doeth the works" (John 14:10).

True humility is the opposite of human ego-based pride,
which tends to close our minds and resist change. Jesus' whole
purpose in this Beatitude was to recreate in us a mind and heart
unfettered and graciously susceptible to the divine impulse and
transforming activity of the Spirit that emanates from within us.

To arrive at the meaning Jesus intended in the words
"Poor in spirit," we have to have some understanding of the
ancient Eastern colloquialisms of Aramaic and, more importantly, of the spiritual symbology that pervaded His message.
More often than not, it is the symbolic and not the literal
meaning that conveys Jesus' spiritual teachings.

"Poor in spirit" means: Devoid of false ego-pride in
what we think we already know, so that we can readily learn
something new and be inspired to a higher understanding. A
good, simple translation would be, "Blessed are the teachable!" This receptive state of mind provides that initiatory
"crack of willingness" that invites the waiting influences of
God's Spirit into our thoughts and feelings and allows divine
guidance and spiritual leadership to begin the reign of the

our lives.

...panish proverb, "Dime de qué presumes y te
...s" ("Tell me what you're proud of and I'll
...are lacking"). In order to surrender our
...efenses, we often must first acknowledge the
inner hollowness and spiritual emptiness - the poverty of spiritual fulfillment - in our lives. So, by "Poor in spirit," Jesus meant to be utterly divested of the pretension of spiritual self-sufficiency and therefore truly spiritually receptive.

One degree of negative deficiency Jesus unmasked in this Beatitude is that which you end up with when you haven't as much as you would have if you had nothing: You are "below zero," "in the hole"! If we are merely ignorant, but willing and receptive, we can readily learn and grow. But it is improbable that we will learn anything about any topic in which we take pride, since we already "know everything that needs to be known." This was the case with those whom Jesus once compared to "whitewashed tombs." They were proud and ego-inflated in the self-sufficiency of their religious knowledge, but destitute in spiritual understanding. They had less than nothing - certainly less than the untrained but amenable multitudes whom they, the religious hierarchy, censored so condescendingly. Yet, it was these provincial folks that were the very people Jesus left Jerusalem to teach.

The Bonds of Pride

One of Jesus' strongest warnings to us - about ourselves - was that special spiritual blindness in which we have achieved a sense of self-rightness and can usually see the faults of others, but not our own. If we feel reasonably secure and gratified with ourselves, we feel no conscious need to change. The "unforgivable sin" is the closed mind and locked heart, blockaded ("damned") against the influence of God's Spirit. By contrast, the gateway to soul growth is the unencumbered mind and the unpretentious heart that is open and receptive to inspiration and spiritual transformation. The truly poor in spirit acutely feel their spiritual need for God, and they are humble in knowing that they do not know everything. In addition, as with children, they are more teachable and eager to learn and improve ("Whosoever shall not receive the Kingdom of God as a little child, shall in no wise enter therein'' Luke 18:17).

Everyone of us is bound, to some degree, by the wrong kind of pride. We may need correction and liberation from our frozen attitudes and fixed expectations. We all may need a way of release from the imprisonment of our limited and wrong beliefs. We each need a way out of the constraint of our domineering, often self-gratifying prejudices and arrogant, intellectual opinions. The surest way to decisive, positive, inner improvement and spiritual transformation is for us to become aware of our ignorance and be willing to go beyond the range of our former concepts and any vested interest that holds us to them.

Perhaps we can see now that these heretofore strange words by which Jesus begins His Beatitudes, ''Blessed are the poor in spirit,'' are a logical, necessary and important first step for entrance into the Kingdom of Spiritual Consciousness through which we make contact with the inner Source of our being and open ourselves to the transforming, perfecting power of God's Spirit in us.

The Turnaround

Everything begins by a change in our consciousness. The conversion comes by realizing our spiritual poverty and recognizing our need for God. It is also the result of becoming teachable and courageous and adventurous enough to challenge and correct our own habitual thinking; by being humble enough to accept into our human ego-construct our spiritual identity and true worth as a Child of God; by being gracious enough to receive new understandings of Truth; and by inviting our original ''Image and Likeness'' Nature to be ''Born again'' in us.

Life offers too much to let our own misconceptions hold us back. The first Beatitude is a prototype of a new start. It reminds us of both the awesome power and the somber obligation involved in one of God's greatest gifts to each of us, spiritual freedom through free choice! It holds out the wonderful prospect, ''Montani semper liberi'': ''Mountaineers are always free.'' It all starts with a transformation in us. At the outset, Jesus presents us with a life-changing dynamic: Blessed are you if you are willing to change and allow your life to expand upward and onward - so get at it!

Chapter Three

An Ache Instead of a Heart?

One of my constant observations as a minister is how many people hurt underneath. Alleviating this could truly change the world. In Jesus' second Beatitude, "Blessed are they that mourn: for they shall be comforted," He disclosed the second major portal of transformation through which we can exit our human bondage and enter the higher life of Spirit that He came to reveal.

The first entrance, "Blessed are the poor in spirit: for theirs is the kingdom of heaven," involved the conscious choice of deliberately surrendering up the self-imposed limits and learning restraints of our human ego-defenses to the enlightening influence of new and higher spiritual understanding. The first Beatitude presupposes a voluntary determination on our part to initiate a change.

God's Grace for our Grief

To all appearances, the second Beatitude, "Blessed are they that mourn: for they shall be comforted," seems to be quite involuntary. It concerns trouble: the problems, pains, afflictions and sorrows that, at times, make life seem difficult and sad. Here, Jesus is revealing that adversity can also introduce us to much larger dimensions of ourselves and serve as a threshold into expanded, enriched living. He is saying that, as much as we would like to avoid them, our adversities tend to engender a blessed receptivity in us towards accepting and embracing the aid and comfort of a Higher Power, especially in a heart that aches.

This Beatitude ties in closely with Jesus' Farewell Address when He said, "Let not your heart be troubled: ye believe in God, believe also in me. In my Father's house are many mansions, if it were not so, I would have told you. I go to prepare a place for you. And if I go and prepare a place for you, I will come again; that where I am, there ye may be also" (John 14:1-3). Here He presents us with a sweeping perception of universal latitude that includes both the immediate, mundane, often illusory, world in which each of us lives at any particular time and then carries us beyond into the ever-expanding Reality of the unfathomed, inexhaustible possibilities of the "Many Mansions" of God. In this Upper Room Discourse we are given a profound message of encouragement, not only for the most familiar external circumstances of our lives, but also in being directed to that special Spiritual Place He prepared for us (the "I AM" Indwelling Christ Awareness) and promised to Appear Again - so overlooked for 2000 years - within our own minds and hearts.

In this extended vision, Jesus was not saying that in this earth-life we would be free from trouble, sorrow and heartache, for He was very familiar with the ways of this world. He knew firsthand - from our point of view - exactly what it is like for each of us to go through the experiences provided by this human world. But more, He understood its purpose and value; and, amid the temporal limitations and difficulties, He recognized the possibilities and opportunities for the soul growth and spiritual development that can come to each of us from consciously working through mourning and surmounting adversity. And framing our lives in their eternal context, He introduced us to a cosmic vision of our existence and a deep center within ourselves from which to live.

Joining Heaven and the Heart

Jesus begins at the Center. He used our hearts to represent this Spiritual Core of our being where our eternal Oneness with God is untouched and unaffected by any of our human beliefs in our separation from God. When Jesus said, "Let not your heart be troubled," He was telling us to establish our consciousness in this strong Spiritual Center ("Kingdom"), which is never involved in anything pertaining to fear, discouragement, pain, death, or any of the negatives of earth-life. Then, as we hold steady here and let our hearts "not be troubled" in any of the troublesome and difficult ordeals that might come our way, we will not only come through the experience but also come up higher.

Even when we do regard this earth as a school-house, we can often feel as though we are enrolled in a curriculum that we don't remember signing up for! What we do not understand is that this life is not, essentially, a good place to have just what we want, when we want it, the way we want it. That is not what it has been designed for. This life was never intended to be our childish idea of a paradise. Neither is it merely a "vale of tears." Rather, it is an ideal place in which to learn and grow, and to thereby serve and unfold our Divine Potential. Jesus knew personally that our normal and occasionally exceptional human experiences will always afford us with ample opportunities to apply this Beatitude. Another comforting aspect of His Good News is found in the understanding that in God's spiritually perfect Creation, mistakes have no permanence, and only the good endures.

So in presenting this second Beatitude, "Blessed are they that mourn: for they shall be comforted," Jesus was proffering and giving meaning and support to the high vision that life on earth is part of our long range spiritual education in the "University of the Universe." And our being here, if we can see it with the eyes of spiritual discernment, is an opportunity for our soul's development and evolution. We each bring into this life our own unique gifts and talents as well as our so-called handicaps in order to attract to us just the right opportunities and special challenges for our optimum personal growth. We also share many things in common.

Jesus knew that the strongest heart sometimes "breaks." And although we differ in so many ways - with different backgrounds, viewpoints, advantages and encumbrances - we all have the one thing in common: sometime, somewhere in our lives, we will all have eyes that fill with tears and an "ache instead of a heart." It is a universal human experience. Even for Jesus, there was ultimately the Cross.

Facing the Hard Things

In fact, from an early age, Jesus was well acquainted with the sorrow and grief of this world. He lived in a time of violence, when life was cheap. When He was an infant, His parents had been forced to flee their native country in order to save Him from Herod's edict to kill all newborn Hebrew children. According to Josephus, coinciding with the time that He was a youth, a Jewish Zealot named Judas Galileus led a raid on a Roman armory about 4 miles from Jesus' home. Roman ven-

and thorough. The town, Sepphoris, was set
s were sold as slaves and, as a warning, the
l with crosses of rebels who were crucified. It
ʝus would have been spared the impact of this
‿‿ιy. If, as a boy, Jesus had seen or heard of a reported
2000 men nailed to death on crosses, He would have grown up
with no delusions about the facts of the human situation.

And as a Jew, Jesus undoubtedly felt the deep, mournful
lamentations that prevailed throughout their religion's sad
history. Jesus also had known personal sorrow. He had lost
his father, Joseph, apparently at a young age. Twice, we read
in the Bible that Jesus, Himself, wept: once for a friend,
Lazarus, and once for His beloved Jerusalem, that would not -
or could not - accept the Truth that He came to reveal.

From His sufferings, Christians have related Jesus to the
Isaiah national messianic prophesy as ''A man of sorrows, and
acquainted with grief'' (Isaiah 53:3). Even more, He was a man
of great compassion. All His life He worked to relieve suffering
and sorrow.

This in itself is very revealing when we remember that in
Jesus' day, people were taught to believe that all suffering was
the result of sin. If a person deserved punishment, he should
get it! This was the old, primitive idea of a wrathful, vengeful God of punishment. But Jesus revealed God in a new light.
The God of Jesus is a merciful, benevolent, loving spiritual
Father. Jesus then translated these same inherent qualities into
the arena of our human encounters (''Ye have heard it said, An
eye for an eye, and a tooth for a tooth: But I say unto you, That
ye shall resist not evil: but whosoever shall smite thee on thy
right cheek, turn to him the other also'' Matthew 5:38,39).

Jesus taught that sin and suffering are not the result of
God's planning (Will) but our failure to bring ourselves into
harmony with His perfect Plan, which is always absolute good.
He came into the world to bring joy, the jubilant
blessings and beatitudes of happiness through the correction of
our shortcomings and guidance into the dormant treasury of our
highest, spiritual possibilities (''These things have I spoken
unto you, that my joy might remain in you, and that your joy
might be full'' John 15:11).

Suffering has become a prominent theme of Christianity. In 333 A.D., the Church focused on the Crucifixion of Jesus. But Jesus' message was not suffering and shame. It was spiritual transformation, the spiritual overcoming and mastery of all the hard and grievous situations and circumstances in our own lives, through the same resurrecting power of Spirit available within ourselves by which Jesus transcended the dreadful ordeal of the Cross.

Why is suffering such an intrinsic part of life as we know it? Ecclesiastes does tell us: "There is a time to weep and a time to laugh." The causes are complex and complicated and we sometimes might think that if we were planning the world, things would be quite different! A little boy once said that he couldn't understand why God put the vitamins in vegetables instead of in cake, pie and ice cream.

Another paradox about "Blessed are they that mourn" is that it actually seems to be congratulating those who are in mourning and grief, seemingly declaring, "Happy are those who consciously are unhappy"! It would seem far more sensible to most people to say, "Blessed are those who are spared the experience of heartache, sorrow and grief."

Today, there seems to be the general notion that we should avoid or escape anything unpleasant - at all costs. We use pills, powders, drinks, entertainment, work, seminars and innumerable other pastimes and abstractions - even religions - to temporarily evade anything disagreeable in our lives. Jesus challenged our prevailing way of looking at all of this. His aim was not to make us miserable for our sins, or to glorify mourning. Nor was He telling us that the secret in life was to avert the hardships. Instead, He wanted us to recognize that everything attending the extremities of "Those who mourn" can become a prime learning experience. He was showing us the opportunity that we each have for growth by the way in which we meet our misfortunes. He would have us use our adversities creatively. Children get right back up from a fall or a skinned knee - after a little crying - and enter full-blown back into the ventures of exploring and expanding their lives.

There is no virtue in unnecessary suffering itself. But absolving the grief of unavoidable pain can point us to the meaning of life, and awaken us to much larger life. The greatest tragedy that can happen to any of us is to suffer the inescapable hardships common to every life and never grow from them.

The most difficult result of suffering and hardship is not the actual pain. People often have a great deal of courage and dignity when faced with pain. It is the apparent waste and sense of futility and uselessness concerning the need to go through the affliction. One of my Minister friend's definition of ''sin'' is ''useless, unnecessary suffering.'' This description presents an insight into the real cure for the widespread use of addictive substances and behaviors as an escape from inner ''hurts'' that seem to have no purpose because we do not yet understand their role.

Sorrow as Holy Ground

But Jesus is telling us in this Beatitude that a transforming dimension is possible with all suffering, that from the worst can come the best and in God's Great Plan for each of us, even our deepest misery and sense of tragedy, loss and separation can be a stage for greater good. As Jacob so dramatically discovered in his banishment from home, adversity and sorrow can become Holy Ground.

Hardship and suffering often drive us to go beneath the surface and shallowness of our lives and tap the spiritual depth and hidden inner Source Jesus identified as God's ''Kingdom'' within us. Adversity often introduces us to our True Selves, and what we can become from our Higher Nature.

Longfellow said, ''The lowest ebb is often a turning point.'' Stars can appear brighter from the bottom of a deep pit than the top of a mountain. And the promise of the inevitable dawn after a ''Dark night of the soul'' is well known to spiritual aspirants. Having an ''Ache instead of a heart'' can induce a state of mind that invites the help and comfort that God can give. It impels us to find our Center.

Affirming and finding that God is with us in our suffering can bring Him very near and make His Presence a Living Reality to us. Sometimes, when things are serious enough, it becomes a moment-to-moment Communion which can lead to a great discovery: our meeting and conquering pain, sorrow and hardship brings power and transformation, for it allows God's greatness to flow into the "vacuum" of our incompleteness.

Through the creative use of suffering, we can become co-partners with God in creating in ourselves an entirely new and higher life - for in a very real sense, God never just mends or patches things up: "Behold, I make all things new" (Revelation 21:5). ("Therefore if any man be in Christ, he is a new creature: old things are passed away; behold, all things are become new" II Corinthians 5:17.)

When we understand Jesus' new way of looking at things, we see that suffering and heartbreak can be given a rightful role in spiritual ascendancy (again, remember the Cross). As it has often been in our greatest individual distress that we find a higher component of ourselves, it has also often been in times of historical hardship that humanity has most rallied its resources and made its greatest advances.

The encouraging assurance in this Beatitude is that from any difficulty can come a Miracle - which is always a breakthrough Christward! The blessed comfort comes with the realization that we are actually made happiest in our lives by knowing the joy of meeting and overcoming challenges head-on, filling our heartbreaks with spiritual meaning and by being transformed "with power from on high" (Luke 24:49).

It is sometimes believed, somewhat in the tradition of La Boheme, that to be a true artist, one must suffer. What is required, along with talent, is maturity. When Joscha Heifetz was a young man, he was a superb technician on his violin, but his music was cold. After he went through some of life's hardships and heartaches, it became warm. It is not necessary to suffer a "broken heart" in order to live a spiritually creative life. But we need a heart that has learned to care and knows how to give.

If mourning is not in itself always our teacher, it can make us seek a teacher. Because we are more responsive to our hearts than our minds, the anguish of a painful emotional blow - more than anything else - can turn us to the real Authority in our lives: the Indwelling Teacher, the Guide, the Comforter, the Holy Spirit. These refer to the spiritual (Whole-making) activity of God's Presence in our minds and hearts.

Throughout our lives, in order to continue learning, growing and expressing the qualities of God (through the Nature of the indwelling Christ) we need heartfelt experiences that require us to increasingly discover and rely upon spiritual help from the depths of our own Center. The first Beatitude prompted us to be willing to change our viewpoint and become receptive and teachable in learning to relate to life from a spiritual standpoint. This is the first step required in accepting a Higher Power that may be summoned at any instant to assist in uplifting us into Higher Life.

Mourning as useful suffering can also help serve the Divine Purpose of our lives by assimilating the pains, conflicts and tragedies into having higher meaning and allowing them to contribute, as stepping-stones, to our regeneration. This is the true meaning of the Cross, a spiritual "Plus-Sign": The victory of the Resurrecting Spirit within and the Ascension of our Hidden Divinity (the Christ in us that is our "Hope of glory" Colossians 1:27) by which our human nature is transmuted into the Divine.

The Meaning of Mourning

It is one thing to experience sorrow and suffering and another to perceive their meaning: first, as a messenger to point out that we are incomplete - all is not well and there is a void to fill - and then, as a means to find the latent resource within to be transformed and made whole. Jesus' promise in this second Beatitude is not to end all sorrow in the experiences of this life, but to assure us of the inherent blessing of new strength and mastery always available in the midst of our troubles.

One of the biggest heartaches in life is in mourning the death of someone we love. This sense of loss imposes a great need for comfort and strength. The full range of human fears and the fundamental belief in separation has at its center the fear of death. We think of death as "the last enemy," an ominous mystery. But it is life that is the great mystery and death is simply a transition, a benevolent release between one stage of life and the next. What we call death on the bottom is birth on the top. For a life well lived, spiritually, death is a graduation, a gateway to Larger Life. The **"last enemy"** is really the **fear** of death - and separation. Paul actually tells us to learn to die daily little deaths to the old so that we can be born to the new.

Grief, which at first is a natural reaction and a sign of our caring and sensitivity, by itself is never a blessing. The promise of this Beatitude is in working through and transcending our grief. To open ourselves to the blessing, we need to recognize that most of our grief is for our own sense of loss. God can then fill the void in us with new understanding about the continuity of life and the true comfort of a certain and abiding trust in His eternal Plans and Provisions.

As we begin to perceive things of Spirit, we discover that Spiritual Truth has been incorporated into many symbolic forms. The first airplane that I learned to fly as an Air Force pilot, the AT6 "Terrible Texan," always had a penny wired into a small hole in the front of the engine. The mechanics explained that it was to pay for our passage across the "River Styx" - in case we didn't make it back. From this, I learned the legend about this mythical river that separates this life from the next. At the time of crossing, the ferryman offers each departing soul a potion which, if they accept, will let them forget all sorrow and failure - but, also, all their joys, triumphs and love.

Our grief is wrapped up in our joy and yoked together with love in the determination of our growth, for an eye that knows no tears knows no tenderness. Yet, we should not give ourselves to unnecessary grief, or hold on and nourish it. The original meaning for Jesus' use of the word "comfort" wasn't merely "to coddle," or "fluff the pillow." It meant to be spiritually buttressed from within and fortified with spiritual strength. It denoted a rebounding heart, restored to blessedness, a heart strengthened with joy and happily awakened to God's Presence.

Of course, death is not the only calamity in life for which we mourn. We also grieve and suffer anytime we feel separated or deprived of a sense of God's Presence. The primary cause of suffering is that we have lost sight of our innate divinity and spiritual origin and built up a belief in separation from God. This is the root cause of the ignorant and wrong thinking that produces the mental images of fear, guilt, anxiety, failure and frustration and binds us to negativity and unhappy conditions.

Yet, there are many things in life from which we suffer or do not enjoy. Among them is the mental anquish and physical pain that tells us we have somehow violated something deep within us, some aspect of our True Nature. There are wrong choices, failures, and the injuries of fear, carelessness and prejudice. There are frustrations, disappointments, rejections and betrayal. There are errors in judgement and misguided ambitions, such as the eventual, tragic realization of the Colonel in The Bridge Over River Kwai: "What have I done?". There is the longing for what might have been. And also for what could or should be except the change requires risk, and facing risk can be agonizing. There is the pain of caring and watching others suffer. And the worst distress of all is the loss of a sense of direction: nothing meaningful to aspire to, no place to go, nothing important to really believe in or live for.

But neither should we assume the passive resignation (especially in metaphysics) that, "no matter what happens," it is always for the best. All things do **not** "work for together good." We must remember Paul's important enjoiner, "to them that love God, to them who are the called according to his purpose" (Romans 8:28). Things **don't** always come out all right! It is a poignant observation that "bad things happen because good people do nothing." It is only with devotion and service to God and His purpose that our lives and circumstances can be truly converted into right outcomes and fulfilled through higher expressions of good.

Jesus would have us use the things that have gone wrong in our lives as opportunities to become victors instead of victims. In this way, sorrow and our mistakes can always be regarded as "blessings in disguise." In my work I have found that most people seriously seek spiritual help initially out of adversity. They may originally hope just to cushion the pain of the consequences of what has gone wrong in their lives, but often find much more! They can find God as a "very present help in trouble" (Psalms 46:1).

Truth Makes Us Free

So, how can we be spiritually strengthened and buttressed from within through our failures, sorrows and losses? Jesus gave us the embracing answer in John 8:32: "Ye shall know the truth, and the truth shall make you free." The remedy for all suffering is to realize that we are spiritual beings, then to do all that is necessary to base our thinking, feeling, words, actions and reactions on Truth. It is, on our part, a discipline. We make a serious commitment in our lives to study, pray, meditate and build into our consciousness a "strong Center" based on the Jesus Christ Truth. This discipleship creates in us a special receptivity and attentiveness to all that pertains to the Spiritual Truth that He came to reveal about our own True Nature, the Hidden Christ in us: "If the Son therefore shall make you free, ye are free indeed" (John 8:36).

Then, in any time of crisis or affliction, major or minor, we apply the Truth we know by holding fast to only those consecrated thoughts and hallowed feelings that abide within the Holy Sanctuary and safety of our inner Spiritual Fortress. ("Because thou hast made the Lord, which is my refuge, even the most High, thy habitation; There shall no evil befall thee, neither shall any plague come nigh thy dwelling. For he shall give his angels charge over thee, to keep thee in all thy ways" Psalms 91:9-11). In having "Let this mind be in you, which was also in Christ Jesus" (Philippians 2:5) we have attained the conditions for an inner stronghold in which our hearts are "not troubled" by anything external. We are "strong in the Lord, and in the power of his might" (Ephesians 6:10).

The leaven of transformation begins with a growing confidence in God's power in us and in the Divine principles and laws of God at work through us. We acquire new values and a new direction. We learn what really counts "when the chips are down" and what is merely superficial in life. As our hearts are strengthened, they are also stretched and softened. We grow more sensitive, understanding and compassionate to others. We become more alive. No longer seeking our Salvation by trying to escape the experiences that life provides, we then enter more fully into all that we can appropriate from the opportunities and awaiting blessings that are always at hand. This is consistent with the very announcement with which Jesus began His ministry: "From that time Jesus began to preach, and to say, Repent: for the kingdom of heaven is at hand" Matthew 4:17).

Within all of this, we make the important discovery that although we cannot control everything that happens to us and around us, we can control everything concerning our Spiritual Destiny that depends on us - inside ourselves - which is what Jesus did on His Cross.

The artist Renoir suffered from rheumatism so much that his painting was a slow and painful process. Perspiration would often break out on his forehead because of the pain, yet he nobly persisted. During one of these periods one of the students pleaded with him to quit, asking him why he tortured himself. Renoir glanced at one of his favorite paintings and replied, "The pain passes, but the beauty remains."

There is, in the Divine Design for this life, both "A time to weep and a time to laugh." Oscar Wilde wrote, "He who can look upon the loveliness of the world and share its sorrow and realize something of the wonder of both, is in immediate contact with divine things and has got as near to God's secret as anyone can get."

We are worth the pains we take with ourselves, because there is something Divine and wonderful in each of us that can come forth, even from the worst trials and the deepest grief that this life can bring. If you doubt this, next time you have "An ache instead of a heart," while you do your human best to work through it, surrender your ache to God and then remember that "Earth has no sorrow that heaven cannot heal" (Thomas Moore); that, in God's Great Plan of Good, nothing is ever finished until it is true and right in God's sight.

Chapter Four

The Mighty and Magnificent Meek

"Blessed are the meek: for they shall inherit the earth" is undoubtedly the most perplexing of the Beatitudes to the modern human. In some ways, the word "Meek" is similar to the first Beatitude's concept of "Poor in spirit." The obvious difference is between the promised objectives: "For theirs is the kingdom of heaven" and "For they shall inherit the earth." They appear as opposites, but are actually two sides of the same coin, under the Principle of Correspondence: "As above, so below - as within, so without."

The Merits of Meekness

First, let us explore what Jesus wanted us to understand about ourselves when He used the word "Meek." To the person of the world, meekness is not regarded as an asset. Instead, it is considered a definite liability in achieving anything decisive in this world in which the prevalent notion is that God helps those who help themselves. (Not only does the modern idea of meekness find little appeal, but less and less alluring is the idea of inheriting the earth!) Few people, including Christians, are really convinced that meekness should be congratulated or applauded, or that the "Meek" are really "Blessed."

The prevailing concept of meekness runs directly counter to our accepted idea of successful, happy living. We admire strength, and we associate meekness with weakness. We say "meek as a mouse" and conjure up images of shy, frightened, submissive people - scurrying into the dark hideaways of life. Or, we say "meek as a lamb," lovesome, but to be pitied for their helplessness (and in the West we don't really like to be characterized as sheep; it invokes our indignation). Few people desire to be meek, or can even conceive of prizing it as a valuable possession. In fact, we would be ashamed to be thought of that way. It carries a "wimp" stigma.

Most important, few people believe that a meek person

shall "inherit the earth." Indeed, they are generally regarded as the least likely. Rather, it is the aggressive and self-assertive who appear to dominate the affairs of this world. Most especially, in the hustle and bustle of the business world and the often fierce competition of the market place, meekness does not make common sense as a quality for success.

Yet the secular misgivings about the down-to-earth practicability of meekness has also been demonstrated to the extreme in the current stratagem of the Religious Right movement. With a professed agenda of political might and right and an authoritarian arrogance as though they owned the copyright to the Bible, they have resorted to intolerance, intimidation, censorship, fear, hatred, misrepresentation and have incited terrorism, vengeance, violence and even murder in a blatant attempt to capture control of "their country" and impose their religious beliefs on everyone.

Part of the misinterpretation of this Beatitude's ennobling ideal lies in biblical translation and part in contemporary interpolation. On one hand, we must not confuse Jesus' meaning of meekness with being self-depreciating, spiritless, fearful, understrengthed, or ineffective. To the contrary, in this third Beatitude, Jesus was extending His summons to a higher, fuller life by now introducing us to a deeper access into our wellspring of inner spiritual resources. In this way, we may further increase our aptitude for expressing our God-gifted talents and abilities and effectively make our most commanding and influential contribution to the world. On the other hand, a religious claim that we are "God's Agents" with a direct line to knowing what God wants is never license to bypass or desecrate the spiritual aspect of meekness with any attitude or action that is unChristlike.

Biblical Role Models

Let's consider some of the important Bible characters who were described as "Meek." In the Old Testament, the best example is Moses, the Great Liberator. He was anything but a despised, unmanly weakling. He was a superb leader: a strong, courageous, firm, sometimes "hot-tempered" rebuilder of an entire nation with the audacity to defy the Pharaoh. Moses also ran a very tight ship in leading the enslaved, weak-willed, complaining, occasionally rebellious Israelites through a forty-year trek of trials and hardships in one of the world's most formidable deserts. He was one of the truly great men of all time. None of the above matches our concept of meekness, yet Moses was described in Numbers 12:3 as among the meekest of men "upon the face of the earth."

The greatness characterized in all of the spiritual heroes and heroines of the Bible - the Patriarchs, the Judges, the Prophets and the Disciples - all correspond to their true meekness. The story of Samson, the biblical strong man, gives us a picturesque Hebrew folk-story example. He was a Nazarite, an "extraordinarily born" child by virtue of a consecration by his mother before his birth to a vow of lifelong devotion and service to the spirit of God. His long hair was a symbol of that dedication. Samson, Hebrew for "Sun-man," is actually a literary prototype of the Hebrew people themselves: strong in number, but confused in purpose and led astray from the Covenant by a distractive attachment to something other than God (Delilah). The spiritual meaning is conveyed in the conclusion of the story when the "regrowth of his consecrated hair" (renewed dedication) restores the strength of his divine energy - under spiritual discipline.

From the beginning in Hebrew literature, meekness was considered the excellent virtue of those who lived their lives devoted to God. As their nation experienced growing conflict and power struggles, often led by men of pride and violence, meekness came to represent inspired leadership by Godly people - those who were spirit-ruled themselves and could submit to God's Will at all times.

We can see this same dramatic inner play in the life of Peter in the taming of the struggling, impulsive side of his human nature. First was his notorious denial of Christ. Next, his blundering misuse of God's power in an early attempt at fear-based leadership resulted in the death of Ananias and Sapphira. Then, with the healing of a beggar at the "Gate Beautiful" in partnership with the Apostle John (love), began the real emergence of Peter's authentic spiritual empowerment and spiritualized leadership.

The Apostle Paul was an aggressive, strong-worded crusader and perhaps the most dauntless missionary in all religious history. Yet, he considered "Meekness" as one of the most worthwhile "Fruits of the spirit" and he pursued it as a priceless and beautiful asset in the enrichment of his own spiritual life.

Jesus was the chief proponent of the value of meekness. The ages have recognized Him as the supreme example of the Christ Life. His life was never a life of resignation or deferment. He proclaimed and used His powers wherever He went, often in the face of opposition. Unlike those who later devised the dogmas and doctrines, nothing that could be experienced in the present was ever postponed for after-death rewards. He had his eyes on a full, spiritually energized life - here and now! (''In earth, as it is in heaven'' Matthew 6:10).

His Gospel shows us how to make the most of earth-life opportunities and open the way to current fulfillment and happiness in the life and bounty which God has given us in this world - as well as all that follows. He pointed us ever ahead. Yet part of His Message reveals how to ''inherit the earth'' in the present. We are now here, by Divine Appointment, to utilize all that God has so graciously provided for those pursuits and objectives. And, as our Great Example and Teacher in this life, He demonstrated that meekness was one of the outstanding characteristics of His Christhood. He said, ''Learn of me, for I am meek and lowly of Heart'' (Matthew 11:29). By sharing His meekness with us, He was sharing His glory. He meant, of course, a dimension and quality of character that is Spirit ruled.

Our Possibilities and Responsibilities

The foundation for all greatness in human life is knowledge of the Spirit of God within each of us. Lasting achievements bring us nearer the dignity and spiritual nobility of the Divine Image that is our True Nature. To live well on earth, we must remember our connection with that which is above. We are essentially spiritual beings, living in an essentially spiritual universe - and we can truly succeed only on the basis of spiritual understanding.

We are here not only for a purpose, but a great purpose. We live in an upward, onward, expanding, whole-making universe. Life is a continuous, unfolding process. Teilhard de Chardin, a Prophet of our age, saw the universal creative process as an evolving whole (''Alpha to Omega'') all reaching and developing in the direction of and coming to fulfillment in the Christed consciousness of human beings. To him, we are the ''leading shoot'' on the cosmic ''Tree of Life.''

Jesus captured this idea in His term "Kingdom of Heaven" (Domain of the universal expansion of Spiritual Potential). He presented life as an evolving process of successive levels and creative stages ("The earth bringeth forth fruit of herself: first the blade, then the ear, then the full grain in the ear" Mark 4:28) - and to Him, the key to the knowledge of life is found in the unity of the whole - "As above, so below" - ("One is your Father, which is in heaven" Matthew 23:9). This unfolding progression for transformation "from on high" and the realization of our universal Oneness (Unity) can be found in the arrangement of His Beatitudes.

The first two Beatitudes are involved with the first level of change: the "crisis entry" into a better way of life. These conditions of entry concern the conscious choice to make a new start and the utilization of our discomfort and pain as an incentive to live a different way. Much of the success for invoking real change depends primarily on our personal determination to adhere to the principles and laws that make transformation possible and persist in the inner discipline that allows it to continue.

We take on a lot of responsibility for ourselves when we enter the process of personal change. For the rest of our lives we need to be accountable for many new areas in the way we live. Much seems to be expected of us and many demands are made on us - mostly by ourselves!

Even "Letting go - and letting God" requires much discipline and a special kind of discretion. There is a certain compulsion of assertive effort - sometimes subtle - that seems to linger in a feeling of the need to take the personal, often sole responsibility in making certain that everything goes right and always works out for what we think is best, long after we are on the path of recovery. Even Moses, a dedicated proponent of the law, failed to make it past the boundary of this presumptive "second bondage," the finitude of human mentality in attempting to "run the show."

This becomes the opportune time to learn that, even in our most devout spiritual endeavors, whatever we establish by the force of personality strength and self-motivation will have to be constantly maintained by that same limited force. When we let down, so does it. On the other hand, anything established by the Higher Power of God's Spirit working through us enlists all the forces of the Universe to back it up and see it through to its perfect outcome ("Not by might, nor by power, but by my spirit" Zechariah 4:6).

A Step Up

In the third of Jesus' Beatitudes, we come up a step and reach beyond our usual faculties. We are presented with a new platform-base of conditions formed by that which was accomplished in the first two Beatitudes combining into a creative synthesis, becoming "greater than the sum of the original parts" and transforming into a third, higher-level "Beautiful Attitude." Thus, in the true criteria for transformation, we shift gears into a new ascendant echelon of spiritual mastery and leadership ("endued with power from on high" Luke 24:49) in which even the rules and laws seem to change.

The most successful far-reaching spiritual recovery programs employ 12 progressive steps, reminiscent of the promised continuum of spiritual guidance and support long ago symbolized in the rungs of Jacob's Ladder - no accident in God's Timely Plan of Redemption. This surfaced into the stream of contemporary human consciousness through the Oxford Group, a movement within the Church of England back to First Century Christianity, from the waiting Spiritual Truth Treasury of the Wisdom Schools of the Ancient Mysteries, the "Golden Thread" of the Perennial Philosophy.

Granted, the ancient teaching that the connecting link in the universe is Mind; that the Ultimate Reality of anything exists as a Perfect Idea in the Mind of God; that true wealth, power, wisdom and mastery are from within and that any enduring change for the good in the outer must be established foremost in the inner domain of mind and heart seems a curious way to "Inherit the earth" to those of us who instead have inherited the Western outer-oriented approach to life. Western people are not usually skilled in the mystical (metaphysical - spiritual) art of the inner life. Therefore, we are not convinced that establishing and administering the external conditions in the plane of human affairs by primarily attending to the condition of our inner consciousness is feasible, much less practical. Paul's insight that "Things which are seen were not made of things which do appear" (Hebrews 11:3) isn't a serious consideration for most of us in getting ahead in life.

The Principle of Correspondence

We have become a goal-setting society. But most of the goals reduce themselves into the material possessions and the self-serving cravings of personal advantage. And whether we recognize it or not, they are mostly the shortsighted exploits of the human ego which at best leads to temporary states of human satisfaction for a few people. Rampant in the intent behind the professed benevolent motivations of commerce, politics, entertainment and much religion is the manipulative use of psychological means, often hidden and unsuspectedly harmful, to bend and mold others into their parochial persuasions and devices. The power-people behind the current crimes-against-humanity and violence-to-nature enterprises and cartels are sometimes otherwise substantial, "morally upright" citizens who go to church, attend concerts and distinguish themselves as community benefactors - showing, as Jesus said, that "As without" is not necessarily an indicator of "As within."

This institutional goal-achieving approach has been applied to our personal lives with myriad variations on how-to-get-what-you-want books and classes under the metaphysical banner of self-improvement and growth-potential. Some of these works, particularly those based on a solid spiritual foundation, are excellent. Many, however, with a self-indulgent egocentric justification that "God wants me to have the best," tend to enlist God in our plans and inform Him of our purposes. They often succeed only in increasing our self-focused anxiety for "getting ahead" and leave us feeling increasingly separated, isolated and vulnerable.

The spiritual imperative of correspondence that is left out or avoided in this egocentric attempt for "Life more abundant" is the unitive meekness-prerequisite: "As above, so below." The Universe is the Self-expression of God. It is not held together from below. From the time of Hermes Trismegistus, it was taught: God's Kingdom is within us - It is governed from on top.

Paul's Classic Conversion

Paul said: "And be not conformed to this world: but be ye transformed by the renewing of your mind, that ye may prove what is that good, and acceptable, and perfect, will of God" (Romans 12:2). He wrote this from rich, personal experience. Paul was born with "a silver spoon in his mouth." He had almost everything that anyone wants in this world and works, prays and strives for all their lives: wealth, power, social prominence, high religious stature and political influence. How proud he must have been as a young man in charge of a troop of Temple Guards leading a mission to Damascus to seize the escaping followers of the disruptive heretic Jesus. Then in the blinding flash of a spiritual experience (knocking him off of his "high horse" and temporarily blinding him to the outer world in order that he might truly apprehend the Inner Light), he lost everything that the external world can bestow.

From that time on, his entire life was assuredly disrupted. Instead of entering Damascus like a conquering hero, he was led in like a blind beggar. He had to escape by being lowered over the city wall in a garbage basket. He was considered a "turncoat" to his fellow Jews, a spy to the followers of Jesus and an impostor by the Disciples. Later, in his Second Epistle to the Corinthians, he recalled that he had been beaten, shipwrecked, robbed, snakebitten, cheated, lied about, arrested and imprisoned, suffered hunger and thirst and cold and nakedness. And that was just "those things that are without." The inner turmoil and suffering were even more painful. Yet as a positive and generative result of Paul's crash-course in humility, he concluded, "For I reckon that the sufferings of this present time are not worthy to be compared with the glory which shall be revealed in us" (Romans 8:18).

Meekness can be our passport to this same spiritual realization. If we can become convinced of the practical as well as the spiritual might and magnificence of meekness, it will become a high-priority goal in our lives - as it has in the lives of all truly great human beings - for the quality that Jesus regarded as meekness is a visa to spiritual greatness.

True Meekness

The Greek word for meekness involved in early translations (Praus) described a wild animal that had been tamed; as a horse is brought under reign and serviceable control - wonderfully represented by the unbroken colt that Jesus rode in the Triumphal Entry. In Hebrew, the formal language of the Jewish religion, it meant "to be molded": given meaningful shape and beauty by a potter. Aramaic, the common language of Jesus' people, expressed the concept of yielding; as mountain goats defer to each other when they meet on narrow passages by one lying down so the other may pass over; or, bending, as a mighty oak bends in the wind. The non-biblical (French) word "Debonair" adds a final touch to the distinctive attributes that true meekness bestows: the graciousness, dignity, consideration, courtesy, compassion and well-mannered congeniality of a gentleman or gentlewoman.

Meekness is an attitude or direction and quality in consciousness that is receptive, patient, nonresistant, and accommodating to the inner promptings of Spirit to come up higher. It is the taming of our "wild side" animal nature (yes, it's there!) through spiritually reinforced self- control. It leaves us free to be molded In His Image ("Until Christ be formed in you" Galatians 4:19). It is the mental flexibility of yielding to the highest ideals ("If ye then be risen with Christ, seek those things which are above...set your affection on things above, not on things on the earth" Colossians 3:1,2). It is to bend to God's Will and Purpose as the highest possible influence for good in our lives ("Nevertheless not my will, but thine be done" Luke 22:42). It is to be true to the spiritual dignity, integrity and holiness of our True Self ("I live, yet not I, but Christ liveth in me" Galatians 2:20).

Perhaps the real distinction between the "Poor in spirit" and the "Meek" is that the former are "teachable" and the latter are "inspirable." They contain much in common, but ultimately they are different.

A disciple is a "learner." When we become interested in Spiritual Truth, unless we are under a carefully guided program of spiritual discipline such as "The Sermon On The Mount," it is our natural propensity to become a "seeker." We search the bookstores, classes and seminars for more understanding. Being a serious Truth Student represents a lifetime commitment. But there can soon be a point of diminishing returns in which we become "overread and underdone." It is one thing to "know about" a Truth, and quite another to actually "realize" it (manifest Its Spiritual Reality) in our lives. It needs to "take" and be converted into a valuable, purposeful living experience or it remains a "headtrip."

By its very definition, inspiration transcends the limits of human reason gained through our intellect and our normal, rational-deductive learning process. But as with Jesus and the Law it does not abolish our intellect, it completes it. Our meekness is concerned mainly with our intellect and the false ego-identity it has invented for itself.

Our intellect functions as an indispensable executor in the rightful administration of certain aspects of our consciousness. Yet the intellect can degenerate into a relentless and, at times, ingenious tyrant, knocking down all challengers. The contest between Moses and the Pharaoh, for example, depicts the resistance encountered in the attempts to free ourselves from the bondage imposed on us and our world by our pride-bound human mentality.

Surrender is almost always regarded as a defeat by the human ego. However, to our soul, it can be a great victory. Jesus constantly challenged us to take a good look at ourselves: at the quality of our motives, the true reasons for our goals and ambitions and the insecurities and fears behind our pretenses and cover-ups. He wanted to move us into a vantage position of one of life's most important and authentic choices, "Bondage or Liberty, Which!" (Lessons In Truth by H. Emilie Cady).

It is through meekness that our total consciousness is prepared for passage across the most formidable barrier in our spiritual path. This is the "second bondage" limitation formed by our intellectual-ego rulership. When we are open to inspiration and can yield to new ideas, we no longer are solely dependent on human logic and knowledge, or live from fixed, habitual attitudes and rigid human plans, or are limited to the competence of our personality level. We are truly free to let God work in our consciousness and change us for the better. We can then enter into the Rulership ("Kingdom") of God.

The Crossover

Those who cross over into this "Promised Land" of awakening spiritual awareness know a new kind of world. They begin to live in a different consciousness. Their thoughts and feelings become attuned to the upward, progressive movement of life. They know that there is a vast amount of knowledge beyond that which we have apprehended with our human senses. They know that our bridge to the infinite is through our God-mindedness. They understand that our human ego-personality tends to isolate us from the "Big Picture" with false desires so instead they learn to value and pursue that which fulfills our genuine spiritual needs.

They accept Jesus' High Vision that we are always bigger in potential than our present selves. They are willing to "let go" and "go beyond" by allowing their personalities to lose the primary place of control and power in their lives. They learn to take their human ego selves less seriously and concentrate their personal interest and fidelity to the emergence of their True Nature. They know that it is the Truth about their Spiritual Identity that "shall make them free" and they dearly value the Divine gifts of nonresistance and forgiveness that release them from the mental and emotional misconceptions and misapplications of that which is basically good.

They appreciate that we are each a "bundle of spiritual possibilities" given the latent ability to carry out God's Creative Plans in the realm of their own consciousness and lives. They learn to draw on inspiration, ideas, strength, power and capabilities that lie beyond their present level of awareness and then harness these possibilities. They are guided by Spirit into new ways to understand Truth and how to apply the principles and laws. As with Paul, they undergo a radical change of ambition. They gain the courage to hold fast in the face of whatever might come with the inner and outer changes that occur in their lives. They are full Apostles: "Spiritual Warriors."

They aspire for a sense of Spiritual Flow and "Divine Order" - the wisdom to do the right thing, at the right time, for the right reason. They also learn when and how to release things entirely to God. They become confident that - in the ebb and flow of the unfoldment of their True Nature - Spirit always meets and helps them exactly where they are (again reminiscent of Jacob's Ladder, ''Surely the Lord is in this place; and I knew it not'' Genesis 28:16). They learn to trust the process. They learn to cultivate more and calculate and manipulate less, ignore trifles and cease to care anxiously what others may think, say and do in opposition to their own guidance and leadings from Spirit (''What is that to thee? follow thou me'' John 21:22).

Their goals shift inward toward new heights of internal achievements: the development of a spiritualized mind, with new ideas, new thoughts and feelings and a new kind of inner mastery. Their visions and the object of their prayer and meditation is aimed not at what they will have and retain for themselves, but what they will become and be able to release for the good of all.

They accept the responsibility for all they can possibly do to invite and support the activity of Spirit to work in and through them, but they are willing to let God be God in them. They always consider Him the Senior Partner in the full time enterprise of being about their ''Father's business'' (Luke 2:49).

Jesus as Model Mystic

Are there such people as these? Indeed there are! They have existed throughout history. The most fitting name for them is Mystics. But in the Western culture, the word ''mystical'' is misunderstood. We are apt to think of mysticism in disreputable terms like ''kooky'' or ''flaky,'' or worse, associate it with infamous offbeat or cultish practices. At best, we are apt to think of a ''mystic'' as an impractical dreamer and ivory-towered visionary who has no real contact with the harsh reality of the everyday world.

The dictionary corrects some of this. Mystical is defined as ''having spiritual meaning, or an experience of the inner light.'' Mysticism is ''direct knowledge of God, spiritual truth, or ultimate reality.''

''The Last Supper,'' first instituted as ''Communion'' by Paul (I Corinthians 10:16), has become a central experience of

Christianity: an inner, personal and private encounter with the Living Presence of God. A language of Spirit is symbology. The Hebrew Testament used the beautiful symbols of "The Holy of holies," "The Secret Place of the Most High" and "The Still Small Voice" to establish both the intimate, sacred inwardness and spiritual authenticity of the direct guidance and sovereign authority of divine revelation in our own individual consciousness. Jesus added the symbolic "Inner Chamber" (Matthew 6:6 ASV) and the more direct assertion, "Howbeit when he, the Spirit of truth, is come, he will guide you unto all truth" (John 16:13).

The history of the formation of the early Church is characterized by enforcing the authority of the Ecclesiastic Hierarchy through minimizing personal inspiration or excluding anyone but those considered "Chosen" as capable of receiving Divine Revelation. Nevertheless, from the beginning, spiritual illumination and intuitive enlightenment has been a recurrent experience for countless individuals.

In his conversation with Nicodemus, Jesus vividly emphasized that being "born of the Spirit" (John 3:8) is the primary precondition to entering the dimension of life that can be lived only from spiritual consciousness. Pentecost and the Christian recognition of the direct influence of the Holy Spirit (the quickening of God's Infinite Intelligence in our consciousness), has Its own history of persistence since this first occurred with the Birth and then Baptism of Jesus, followed by the dramatic awakening of the original Disciples. William James's The Varieties of Religious Experience and Bucke's Cosmic Consciousness have traced and distinguished some of the classic examples of the spiritually awakened.

Yet the life-changing experience of awakening spiritually has taken many creative forms other than that delineated or prescribed in the authoritarian tenets of orthodox religions. Countless transcendent experiences central to Jesus' spiritual Gospel have occurred outside any formal religious context. The aforementioned Twelve Steps, originating from the spiritual experience of A.A.'s Founder, Bill W., incorporates into the Twelfth Step the unequivocal affirmation: "Having had a spiritual awakening as the result of these Steps" - and this has been confirmed in the transformed lives of increasing thousands.

In recent years there has been an increased interest in mysticism. A 1978 national survey showed that more than one third of the American public has had a mystical experience. But because such transcendental occurrences are not within accepted religious convention and we don't have the vocabulary to explain the phenomenon, the average mystically awakened person doesn't discuss it with anyone and is often reluctant or even afraid to talk about it.

Mysticism is closely bound to Spiritual Truth and the mystical experience is always spiritual and transformational. This brings us to the definition of a "Mystic": someone who has entered into and begun to live from a spiritually transformed consciousness - **"Spiritual Eagles"** on the rise.

What is the "As above - so below" correspondence between spiritual consciousness and "Inheriting the earth?" Again we turn to the "Mystic" for the answer. "Wherefore by their fruits ye shall know them" (Matthew 7:20). If we were to list the more famous Mystics of history, we would probably be amazed how practical and competent they have been in their lives. In fact, we would find that they were often the creatively-inspired geniuses that have changed the world for the better and brought it forward. They have given us the inventions, scientific discoveries, philosophy, religious inspiration, government ideologies, great art, literature and music, humanitarian attainments and much of our courage, honor and humor.

Inheriting the Earth

The earth belongs to those who know how to inherit it. The first knowledge required is to know what it is that we inherit. Very few people really know. "Belong" here does not mean to "possess" or "own," attitudes that invariably separate us from others and our own highest interests by bending things to our desires and personal will. "Practical Christianity" to the modern mystic Charles Fillmore meant simply to use the experiences of life to demonstrate the teachings of Jesus ("...that ye may prove what is the good, and acceptable, and perfect will of God" Romans 12:2).

What we inherit is the privilege of extracting all the good we can out of every experience available to us. We also inherit the ability to gain the utmost value from every lesson that comes by unswervingly using the Spiritual Truth we know at every opportunity and allowing It to work and unfold through us and become a tangible expression in our lives.

We grow in the direction in which we express ourselves. We always bring forth and fulfill the best in ourselves by letting Truth have its way in and through us, not for our personal gain and aggrandizement, but for the common good of all. The earth "And the fullness thereof" is entrusted to our care. A good companion word to "meekness" is "stewardship."

There was a tradition in the Roman Empire that when a General returned after a successful campaign and entered Rome with a triumphal entry, a slave stood behind him and continually whispered in his ear, "Glory is fleeting." This is what meekness first whispers to us. It then invites us to "Lay up for yourselves treasures in heaven" (Matthew 6:20), for whatever we establish in Heaven (creative, spiritual consciousness) from the right use of our experiences on earth, is ours forever. And we, in turn - as spiritual, creative humans - leave a wonderful legacy for all humanity.

Gandhi, who learned the principle of nonviolence from "The Sermon On The Mount," provided one of the major examples for all time on how to be a Creative Spiritual Overcomer. In an entirely different way, George Washington Carver demonstrated true meekness by opening himself humbly to serving the good that the common peanut could be to humankind. There are legions of self-forgetting, spirit-ruled, not-conformed-to-this-world people who are getting the most out of this world and giving it back increased by serving the highest they know. One of my favorites is Mother Teresa. Once, when she began to expand her humanitarian work, another religious group told her that they wanted to support her in prayer. They asked her what she really would like to have them pray for. She answered, "Pray that we don't get in the way!"

Blessed are the mighty, magnificent meek, for they will

inherit all that the earth really has to bestow!

Chapter Five

A Taste for Life

In a creative progression, Jesus' fourth Beatitude, "Blessed are they that hunger and thirst after righteousness: for they shall be filled," presents to us an exhilarating new facet of our spiritual development. Jesus knew that we hunger and thirst for far more than the world can give. He now summons us to consolidate our deepest Divine Urges and Spiritual Drives, as well as our everyday human dreams and longings, and add a new dimension of enthusiasm, passion and momentum to bolster us in our soul's quest.

Bible writers often employed food and drink as symbols for those intangible essentials that nourish the soul. Jesus, as had Melchizedek in the "possessor of heaven and earth" blessing of Abram (Genesis 14:18-2O), used bread and wine to represent the Elements in the Communion experience by which we appropriate Spiritual Truth into our consciousness and assimilate It into the activity of our lives.

The Blessings of Spiritual Hunger and Thirst

In this Beatitude, Jesus tells us how to marshal our inner drives and potentials. He offers a refreshing formula of fulfillment for converting our misdirected and dissipated appetites and inclinations into His Divine Strategy for "Life more abundant."

What are the basic drives and motivations that shape our lives? The wise old Greeks placed over their temple entrances, "Man, Know thyself." In a scientific attempt to do just that, modern researchers in psychology have evolved up a ladder of their own discoveries. It started with Freud and his view that the instinctive root-cause (subconscious) motivation in our lives is the natural "biological (sex) drive." Adler advanced it up a notch to "power"; Jung to "religious archetypes"; Frankl to "meaning"; Tournier to "adventure."

Abraham Maslow has given us a corresponding hierarchy of needs. The basics are food, shelter, comfort, rest and recreation. It evolves upward through social contacts, communication, privacy, freedom, enjoyment, new thresholds, correction, music, poetry, art, beauty, peace, love, sharing, spiritual awareness and the experience of the Divine Presence. Once we have climbed up a rung, we rarely go back down. If need be, we are inclined to sacrifice a lower need for a higher (for example, people and nations will give up the basics of food, shelter, etc. for freedom).

Long before, Jesus revealed that God had placed His Nature ("The only begotten from the Father" John 1:14) in every one of us accompanied by an insatiable longing for the Parent Spirit. He also concurred with the ancient Psalmists that we have a built-in spiritual hunger to experience and express God in our lives ("For he satisfieth the longing soul, and filleth the hungry soul with goodness" Psalms 107:9) and a divine thirst to know God's Presence ("As the hart panteth after the water brooks, so panteth my soul after thee, O God" Psalms 42:1).

A good and wholesome appetite and a hearty thirst are blessings to treasure. They are a mark of life and a sign of good health, as well as signals of needs. Most people are interested in what they eat. Hunger and thirst are normal, healthful functions of growth and a source of enjoyment and delight. The loss of either one is a flag of danger.

Yet we hear Jesus' Temptation Scripture, "Man shall not live by bread alone" (Matthew 4:4). This is an indicator of the wonderful privileges that God has granted only to humankind. The enjoyment of beauty, aesthetics and adventure, the pleasure of creative expression, the appreciation of the elevating and enlightening qualities of high ideals and values and the capabilities for embodying the virtues of righteousness are sacred gifts. These divine endowments are where the thrill, the splendor and the glory of the blessedness of living and the higher happiness of the Beatitudes come from.

Underneath the exterior of even the most profane personality is a thirst for the experiences of these exalting God-qualities in their lives and a hunger for full knowledge about the higher Will and Ways of God. None of us shall ever be truly satisfied with anything different, or partial.

The person who loses his or her appetite for physical food is to be pitied, but more grievous is the calamity of losing an appetite for the "Bread of Life." Many of the tragedies in our lives come from misunderstanding the true longings and desires of our souls. As a result, we dispel our energies and squander our resources by pursuing the false ambitions and goals of lesser appetites. We eventually "hit bottom" and, like the Prodigal Son who "would fain have filled his belly with the husks that the swine did eat" (Luke 15:16), we grovel in a life that should be a spiritual feast. Most of our restlessness, confusion and emptiness is from developing an appetite for even "second best."

One of the most reassuring promises in the Bible - repeated often - can be found in the words: "And it came to pass." Many things in this life change and pass, thank God! In the process, we are given the continuing opportunity to have our transient "trial and error" mistakes corrected and our temporal challenges overcome. This deliverance and restoration of even "the years that the locust hath eaten" (Joel 2:25) is the combined objective of the first three Beatitudes.

But in this fourth "Beautiful Attitude," Jesus would then have us heighten our spiritual perspective by learning to recognize, esteem and aim for those enduring things that have the "Stuff of Eternity" by nurturing a taste for treasures that last ("the water that I give him shall be in him a well of water springing up unto everlasting life" John 4:14).

The words that Jesus used for this spiritual "Hunger and thirst" were drastic words, denoting "hunger" to the point of starvation and "thirst" to the extent of dehydration. This emphasis was given in a poverty-stricken desert area where the extremity of the meaning was not likely to be lost. With these metaphysical images, Jesus also sought to show the heightened degree of commitment and dedication on which our continued advancement into the Life of Spirit depends. The point is, our spiritual "Hungers" and "Thirsts" are vital, elemental Divine Impulses for our spiritual fruition and they are integral to the fulfillment and glorification of the Divine Pattern in which we

were created ("Christ in you, the hope of glory" Colossians
1:27). And Jesus related these words to "righteousness."

Righteousness'' Defined

The term "righteousness," like "Poor in Spirit," or
"meekness," has fallen into bad company and come to have an
unfortunate association as a frightfully pious word. It invokes
repelling effigies of self-styled professional religionists: self-
righteousness at its worst - the one human trait that Jesus
attacked head-on. In this alliance, who wants to be "righteous"?

Perhaps the word "goodness," in its relation to the
Omnipresent **Goodness** of God, "the Highest **Good**" or "all
things working together for **good**" conveys to us more nearly
the right concept. Jesus made it easy to believe in goodness.
In Him it was a supreme virtue, something we can all admire.
His goodness was from within, an extension of his Christhood.
Goodness is, therefore, a quality of Spirit; and for us, it can be
a sense of God-ness (Oneness) that nourishes us from the
Source, the Wellspring of God's Spiritual Presence that indwells
us. In this Beatitude, Jesus talked about Goodness (Spiritual
Rightness) as though it were the essential, inner food and drink
of life itself.

In the ancient Hebrew, "righteousness" meant compliance with the Mosaic Law. Jesus greatly broadened and
extended it to include right <u>thought</u>, right <u>feeling</u>, right <u>motive</u>,
and right <u>purpose</u> as well as right action as avenues for our
good: right in Principle ("As above, so below") and rightly
aligned with the Law of Mind Action, ("As within, so without").

Jesus taught that life is lived from within - outward.
Everything in Creation unfolds from center to circumference.
This is especially important to understand when working with
the Spiritual Causes and Forces at work behind the scenes in the
Creative Process. Jesus clearly stated that "The kingdom of
God is **within** you" (Luke 17:21). His emphasis, therefore,
always concerned our inner life. He concentrated exclusively
on internal causes of thoughts and feelings rather than external
effects of situations and circumstances, knowing that when we

are right within, the outer life will take care of itself: "But seek ye first The kingdom of God (God Consciousness), and his righteousness (right expression); and all these things shall be added unto you" (Matthew 6:33). Jesus centered the main responsibility of our lives in attending to our consciousness. He constantly stressed the "care and feeding" of our minds and hearts. Put simply, "righteousness" is a right relationship with God, first within, then without. From the ancient Egyptians, it was taught:

"The outward from the inward roll,
And the inward dwells in the inmost soul."

When we "hunger and thirst after righteousness," we are responding to a deep desire in the soul to bring forth, from within ourselves, a corresponding life integrating right inner knowing and right outward doing. First, our minds and hearts are filled with an awareness of God which then allows the Spirit of Truth to find expression through us as the fulfillment of the Divine Will for our lives. Jesus is telling us that the great blessings from this "Beautiful Attitude" come from desiring to uphold right consciousness above all else.

The Gospel throbs with invitations and examples that can quicken us with the thrill of the spiritual adventure of actually living out the promises of Jesus. He knew what is possible for us and His promises and blessings are all achievable!

Creativity

Jesus changed our perception of our potential. From His perspective, every human being is designed to be creative. To Him, we are each a universe in miniature, a microcosm of the Cosmic Creative Process. The "human" of us is a highly creative state of our existence. A main function in this stage of our eternal identity is to affirm the Creative Spirit through a fully creative life. The ways in which the Universal Creative Process can work through a human life are as wide as life itself.

God has shared with each of us the power to create. All creativity is essentially an affirmation of Spirit. It is the ability to manifest spiritual qualities and bring into existence something that has not existed before, the birthing of something original. It is often regarded as the special prerogative of the artistic, but it is a universal human faculty that can operate in every area of human activity. It is always a voyage of discovery and newness. It is the highest form of human existence and it is meant to be enjoyed and participated in by all. Creativity is actually the art of generating our Essential Self, and is, therefore, the key to wholeness and well-being.

To "Know thyself" is to realize the creative endowments that God has vested in us and the importance that cultivating our creativity can make in our own spiritual development and the contribution that we can make for the good of the whole. Holistic self-knowledge especially introduces us to our inner life, a world of its own and the formative realm of our creative activity.

Every person carries within himself or herself "sealed orders" involving his or her unique gifts and capacities with which to specialize the activity of Spirit in specific expressions. Thus God distributes talents throughout the human race for the greatest benefit of all and gives each of us a vital role in the Great Plan of Good. We need only be made aware of our creative possibilities and understand their significance to quicken the powerful influence that Spirit can work through our humanity, including any of our present limitations, to develop all our talents into a Creative Partnership with God individually and collectively.

Let's explore the Creative Process in the individual. The fountainhead of a creative life is **intuition**. Its Divine Origin (virgin conception) is in the Silence of the innermost part of our Soul, the birthplace of our spiritual "Hungers and thirsts." They begin as irrepressible desires Divinely Impulsed from beyond the border of our human consciousness (the domain of the "Unknown God"). Often, they are first perceived as a wordless yearning or vague excitement, perhaps a hunch or intimation of some unforeseen good or, as yet, uncogitated thought or unconceived idea. The Native Americans have an intriguing word for this, "Nagual": anything that can't be named. Intuition points to the unknown, but it is always mysteriously bonded to the right outcome of our true God-given desires.

This mysterious creative power that stirs our special endowments and inspires guidance, wisdom and spiritual empowerment is generally named the "Spirit of God" (the Lord) in the Old Testament and the "Holy Spirit" (Counselor) in the New Testament. It is also referred to as "The love of the Spirit" in Romans 15:30 and the "Spirit of promise" in Ephesians 1:13. As an authentic agency of the "Abiding" Christ within each, It is characterized by John as the "Spirit of Truth." It is also entitled Christ Consciousness, Cosmic Consciousness, Spiritual Consciousness, Illumination, Enlightenment and the Inner Light in Mystics. It is called "inspired genius" in those who distinguish themselves as inventors, philosophers, artists, musicians, poets, authors, humanitarians, educators, scientists, and leaders in government, industry and commerce. Sometimes it is even regarded as eccentricity or whimsy in "common folks."

The intuitive stage is spontaneous. Because It "bubbles up" from a Source beyond the curtain that veils the cosmos, it is not something we can control, or produce by will. The conditions favorable for its inception and unhampered, free-flowing development can be invited and cultivated only by a still, receptive state of mind that allows the Spirit to reveal Itself. The art of meditation, by which we establish an undistracted inner center, is one of our most effective ways of preparing our minds to appropriate and assimilate the Spiritual Impulses that set the creative activity in motion and keep it going.

Its secret influences ("leaven") then give rise to inspired **feelings** which, through the less restrictive language of archetypal symbols, relate to discernible spiritual meaning and take on a personal sense of value and purpose. This subjective, emotional stage is where we also generate our enthusiasm, from a Greek word meaning "to feel God within ourselves."

These inspired and emotionally enriched images - nourished by imagination and visualization - are then introduced into the intellectually conditioned phase of our mind. Through rational **thought**, intelligent planning and deliberate, freewill choices, the original intuitive perceptions are formed into vitalized concepts. These can then manifest into the practical and serviceable applications of tangible expression. Prayer, in all of its creative height and depth, can interpenetrate each stage of the Creative Process, spiritually enhance every quality and escalate every faculty and function involved.

"Creative Blocks"

The inner obstacles that may be encountered in the process are a result of the complex of human hopes, dreams, ambitions and needs that tend to pull in different directions and perhaps lead our original divinely creative "hungers" and "thirsts" astray.

As a result, most of us develop our own version of the so-called artistic "creative block" and gravitate toward pursuing eclectic, materialistic "life-styles" rather than creating real lives. We ignore the alluring spiritual resources and capabilities that God has placed in us for both our benefit and delight. Instead, we eventually tend to settle into or resign ourselves to uninspired, often humdrum living with little credible purpose or meaning. Then we attempt to fill the emptiness with a vicarious and fictional existence through T.V., movies, sports and by escaping into all sorts of diversions outside of ourselves through alcohol, drugs, careers, relationships, sex - often junkfood for the soul that is the modern Prodigal's "husks." All of this masks one of life's most uncreative stalemates: boredom.

The true adventure of life doesn't really begin until we connect it to that mighty Impulse that surges within each of us to pursue and enact our own unique Divine Destiny which, as the mystical poet Shakespeare says, "shapes our ends, rough hew them how we will." This is the great adventure of God, the God within ourselves.

There is an almost instantaneous uplift, joy and renewing power in committing ourselves to a higher sense of loyalty to our own Divine Endowments. It is a reprieve from any sense of separation and bondage to be gripped by something greater than the confines of our present selves. The secret of integrating and mobilizing our lives for growth and fruition is in choosing a cause that commands the best that is in us, something that we believe in with "all our hearts," and then in giving ourselves to it with all our mind and strength. It opens the way to true fulfillment.

Boredom, dissatisfaction and emptiness in our lives, indications that we are living far below our capacities, usually come from noncommitment ("If you know these things, happy are ye if ye do them" John 13:17). Jesus' promises will remain unfulfilled for us until we risk commitment to those Divine Desires that God has placed in us to keep us on an everlasting quest for the fullness of what we were created to be. And as certain as any law, if we don't commit ourselves to something beyond what we are presently doing, we get committed to nothing more than we now have. An example:

"Here lie the bones of Nellie Jones,
For her, life held no terrors,
She lived and died an old maid,
No hits, no runs, no errors."

One of the most effective methods for committing the hungers and thirsts of a more real and rich inner life into an ennobled life of creative transformation and fulfillment can be gained from a profound observation of Teilhard de Chardin about the eternalness of the Creative Process. He reflected that in the infinite vastness of the Macrocosm, which extends far beyond our time-bound human ability of understanding, even our contemplation of Its enormity can overwhelm us with the futility of it all. He said that the secret instead is to develop a taste for life now. (When you think about it, most people who have such grave concerns about "Eternal Life" often don't know quite what to do with themselves on a rainy Saturday afternoon).

The Message of Jesus emanates from the first major announcement of His Ministry - that God's Kingdom exists now ("The kingdom of heaven is at hand" Matthew 4:17). Its blessings are fully available in the present. Returning to His "Upper Room" Communion enactment, we see that His symbols of "Bread" and "Wine" are directly related to His concept of "Daily Bread."

The Eternal Now

In the "Lord's Supper," Jesus offers us a way to spiritualize our everyday lives and live in direct contact with the Transcendent that can be revealed in the commonplace. Although it is well beyond the "loaves and fishes," the secret is found in the "here and now." In presenting us with the symbolic Table of Life and the Bread and Wine of Spirit, He is inviting us to partake of the Sacred Presence and the Transforming Power of Creative Consciousness that is always available. It is an experience and celebration of the Presence of God in the present time and place.

Jesus presented life as an experience in evolving our potential. His Message combined a past, present and future orientation. Our fulfillment is achieved by growth and unfoldment, and the process always leads us ahead. We can't imagine a life without a future.

The past, as a treasury of recollection, is incorporated into the present as a dynamic resource of experience for the birthing of an optimum creative future. In the Communion, Jesus created the highest possible positive influence for the future out of the past with His words, "This do in remembrance of me" (Luke 22:19). We are to especially preserve for the future all the understanding, qualities and attributes about life we can gain from the past through our incomparable spiritual legacy of His Life and Teachings.

But we are to keep our attention on what is "at hand." The past can offer up its total best in the present time. The future can also exist as an all-good possibility in the present. The point of determination and control in life converges into the ever-present now. "Now" is the moment of freedom and the time of transcendence from all the mistakes of the past and all the fears about the future. It can be a wonderful safety zone in which we can maintain a moment-to-moment peace. Our focus of power is in being in and mastering the moment.

The future is born out of the now and the capacity to make changes resides in the now. Now is the moment of causation for everything that lies before us. Life can be lived only in the present moment. When we appreciate where we are and are glad we are there, we enter a new sense of life. Teilhard concluded that the greatest glory of a human is to be the fulcrum of spiritual accomplishment and the bridge to higher good in the Universal Creative Process. Our role is to provide a mind and heart through which the activity of God can work. We do this best by remaining as God-oriented as possible in whatever is the present focus of our attention in the present moment. The moment becomes Sacred and Holy. A new force begins to express itself.

Jesus is telling us to be here now, fully alive to the present moment. In reminding us of our "Daily Bread," He is disclosing that God meets us at the point of our needs, and as with our physical food and drink, our higher "hungers and thirsts" can only be assimilated and satisfied in the present. We cannot force the appropriation or the progression. When working with the hidden rhythms of destiny and spiritual perfection, fulfillment is more often "timing" than time. All our feelings of fulfillment will be experienced as the goodness realized in the blessed time of "this moment."

The Bread and Wine of Spirit

A taste for life is developed by cultivating a good appetite for that which is "Eternal." The Eternal Aspects of Creation are not limited to duration in time, but are the imperishable, indestructible, unchanging qualities that exists outside of time. Paul called on us to live "according to the eternal purpose which (God) proposed in Christ Jesus our Lord" (Ephesians 3:11). This is found in the Spiritual Ingredients and Consciousness of the Christ Nature: "I AM the bread of life: he that cometh to me shall never hunger; he that believeth on me shall never thirst" (John 6:35). This is what we "eat" - The Bread of Christ Qualities. This is what we "drink" - The Wine of Christ Consciousness. This is how we appropriate the Eternal Attributes and ordinary daily existence. This is the Christ Way of inward fulfillment and everlasting satisfaction for every prevailing human need.

The greatest of all adventures is to live on the crest of the wave in the "Eternal Now" realizing that "For this purpose I was brought to this time." This is qualitative time, God-filled, life-altering time in which we are fully alive in the moment, absorbed completely in the "here and now," totally interested in the eternal significance of what is currently present, living directly from our spirituality and entering into larger dimensions of being. Even in "Snatching the Eternal" out of the clutches of the worst of times can make them among the "best moments of our lives." With spiritual awareness, every moment becomes wondrously new and original. This is the ''Living water...the (inner) well of water springing up unto everlasting life'' (John 4:10,14) from where the spiritual rapture and joy of life come.

The Communion mystically unifies our inner and outer lives at the center. Jesus gave us the paramount means for relating our deepest Divine Hungers and Thirsts to the perennial needs of our lives by touching the present moment as much as possible and drawing forth all the nourishing good that it contains. With Brother Lawrence, we are recreated by being born moment by moment into the Presence of God. Jesus would have us dauntlessly face the present moment with anticipation and aspiration, and realize that it is always the most important moment in our eternal life. For in it we can be as new and young as the moment we were created - experientially ''Born again''! And, in the process, we can be filled with the supreme nutriment of life: an abiding sense of God's Eternal Presence.

Chapter Six

Of Knights and Angels

All systems of spiritual growth have provisions for reviewing and testing the progress of the Aspirant. This fifth Beatitude, halfway up the Path, is the Sermon on the Mount's "midterm exam." And it is especially important as a check for hidden blindness or "omissions" amidst our maturing spiritual discipleship. It is perhaps the most arresting and energizing of all the Beatitudes.

The forceful precept, "Blessed are the merciful: for they shall obtain mercy," can be challenging when taken seriously. It can bring to mind our own lapses of hasty and unfair judgements, criticism, gossip and character slander and our remoteness or indifference to the serious difficulties and heartaches of others. By pulling us up short, it can tend to make us recognize and appreciate the mercy - especially from God - that we have often received for the same kinds of shortcomings, faults and unfortunate dilemmas of our own that we have condemned or patronized in others.

Blessed are the Merciful

The genius in which Jesus presented this "Beautiful Attitude" can be seen, in part, by the fact that He could say just a few words and, like the spiritual rungs of "Jacob's Ladder," convey meaning on so many levels. Often the first accomplishment His words achieve is to halt us right in our tracks with the recognition of the ways in which we have still gone along with worldly "conventional wisdom," rationalizing and fooling ourselves about what we have allowed to really go on in our lives. Then, by providing a moment of insight and spiritual honesty, He gives us the alternative: The promise of renewed opportunity, followed by increasing inspiration, guidance and the assurance of far more good yet to come - as we continue to earn the right.

The translation "merciful" is derived from two Hebrew

words, ''rahum'' and ''hesed.'' They are both found in the Torah. Integrated, they express a more comprehensive and expressive meaning than ''mercy'' and represents one of the richest traditions in the Hebrew's religious history. ''Rahum,'' from the root ''rehem,'' means ''womb''; thus connoting the altruistic affinity and tenderhearted compassion that mothers feel for an unborn or recently born child - before sleepless nights and aggravation set in. ''Hesed'' connotes a more encompassing loving-kindness, extended beyond intimate family and close friends to a wider circle of strangers who may be neither weak, ailing nor needy; they may even be successful and powerful.

There is also a gamut of multiple meanings and implications in the Torah. It extends from the foundation layer of Jewish spirituality of enlightened individuals to the carrot and stick approach required by the unenlightened masses to guide them into higher understanding and lead them towards eventual spiritual awakening and growth.

Over the centuries, the religious concepts of the masses about God slowly evolved from a primal belief in a severe, exacting creditor who visited punishment for every offense into the sublime concept of a loving, spiritual Father, as revealed in Jesus' spiritually generic message. (In an inverted evolution, ''Satan'' was first introduced in the Bible in the most positive way through the story of Job - not as a villain, but as a servant of God. His role was that of ''examiner'' who would test people in their readiness for the next grade of life. The legendary ''Fallen Angel'' concept evolved much later.) It was in the book of the Prophet Hosea that the level of enlightened understanding about a God of mercy was openly revealed to the religious majority of our ancient Biblical ancestors. From that disclosure in the Hebrew Bible, ''mercy'' came to be accepted by the Hebrews populace as a key quality in describing God's gracious disposition toward them. Jesus' portrayal of mercy brought to full light the broadest and highest understanding of the universal compassion, total beneficence and boundless grace that God endlessly extends to all people as beloved children.

Because people often tend to reflect in their own lives whatever characteristics they believe that God possesses, ''mercy'' also grew to mean the kindred attributes of care, concern, generosity and benevolence that humans should render to one another, especially to the weak and helpless. This is the essence of the Golden Rule, which is found in all major religions. This principle reaffirms this Beatitude's pronouncement that the way in which we choose to treat others notifies the universe of the way in which we can expect to be treated in return.

"Hesed" came to mean "put yourself in the other person's shoes," literally to "get inside another person," feel what they feel, know what they know and experience exactly what they are experiencing. This concept represents more than sympathy or sentimentality, which are often weaker and transient. "Hesed" is a deliberate identification with another, an empathy of oneness in which we try to sense and share some of their inner life.

Largehearted Mercy

This kind of mercy requires us to refine and sharpen our insight and learn to listen and discern more of what is really involved in someone else's life. It requires that we try to understand what someone else means rather than just what he or she says. It is a deeply caring involvement, centered in the highest type of human love and tender regard for others that is now most often expressed by parents to their children. This kind of mercy takes time and experience, because to mercifully accept, understand and share in another person's life, we must have done some living ourselves.

In Jesus' time, as often now, the older "avenging God" notions of revenge and vindictiveness were more apt to prevail than those of forgiveness, compassion and kindness. Jesus' emphasis on "mercy" was at sharp issue with the lower common denominator values of the general populace. Often, rather than being endorsed, mercy was regarded as weak and unattractive. The Romans loathed pity. And at times the Jewish majority could have less than enlightened provisions for real compassion even among their own people, as seen in the frequent criticism of Jesus in His regard for human needs over the "letter of the law" and their merciless treatment of Him personally. As a result, the Pharisees, with some rather unmerciful doctrinal "bad press," have collectively become the classic stereotype of religious "stiff-necks" who applaud self-sufficiency and have no tolerance toward those who failed to meet their standards.

But such spiritually devastating traits are far from eradicated in many present religious leaders and congregations. Entire dominations still cling for a base of support to antiquated, negative religious belief-systems. Robert Louis Stevenson wrote: "There is an idea abroad among mortal men that they should make their neighbor good. One person I have to make good: myself. But, my daily duty to my neighbor is much more nearly expressed by saying that I have to make him happy - if I may." Even more arresting are the remarks of a trial lawyer. "'Good men,' in the sense which the word generally indicates, have so little sympathy with 'bad men' - and are so seldom kind. Being 'good men' themselves, they think the law should make everyone else good." He concluded: "If I am ever on trial, I hope I do not have a jury of 'good men,' for 'good men' are convictors."

We all recognize the type: not righteous, but self-righteous, harsh and unmerciful in their judgement of all those who do not measure up to their self-appointed determinations and convictions. Jesus censured these characteristics in the religious leaders more strongly than any other inglorious human trait.

True mercy is a natural expression of love. Jesus made it clear that love, kindness, forgiveness and goodwill are greater than and always take precedent over the letter of the law. God's laws never interfere with our expression of the highest and best qualities of which we are capable at any time. They are guides and aides for our growth. The merciful heart does not come to us full blown. It grows by our use through the law of giving and receiving. There is no other way to build a merciful heart except through opening ourselves to the magnanimous release of God's mercy within ourselves, and in return expressing merciful thoughts, feelings, words and actions in our lives. We cultivate and establish a merciful heart when we base all the relationships of our lives on the Spiritual Pattern of God's mercy that was revealed in the life of Jesus. From Him, we derive the teachings of the Fatherhood of God, the Brotherhood of man and the ideals of doing justly, kindly and lovingly in our everyday living. In Him we have always had the perfect example of what it is to be merciful.

The Early Church

The Church had a humble beginning. For several generations it was under threat from both the Jews and the Romans. These Early Christians were closely bonded by their courage and their impassioned support of each other. Divisions, however, developed within the Church over differences in some of the teachings. Aggressive efforts were used to build a strong organization and centralize control. To convert the uneducated masses, early leaders taught believers to dwell on the darkness of their own nature and to consider non-believers as "enemies." The main function of Christian converts was not to improve or elevate themselves, but to "defend the faith."

Rather than advancing the Fatherhood of God and the Brotherhood of man, time after time the Church promoted and enforced further separations and fragmentations - which regrettably has been characteristic of most of the resulting subdivided denominations ever since. After the conversion of the Roman Emperor Constantine, the Church eventually took the place of Rome in the political and military conquest of the Western world. As Christianity spread throughout Europe, Jesus' concept of mercy as a desirable and even necessary attribute of a God-centered life had to go up against the brutality and chaos of the Dark Ages and also make its way through the militancy and narrowness of a dominantly empire-building theology.

The Noble Knights

Eventually the higher qualities that the Church had originally sought to represent found a strange champion among the warriors themselves - Knighthood. Knights were basically soldiers on horseback who fought to protect the interests of feudal landowners. Anyone could be a Knight if he could ride a horse and fight. These warriors grew strong and began to band themselves together into a loyal fighting brotherhood. They rallied to a religious cause during the Crusades, but again they were soldiers in a military campaign of conquest attempting to wrest the Holy Land back from the Moslems. But in the mysterious ways of God, the bloody combat of the Crusades served as a turning point for the contribution the Western World was destined to make toward human progress.

Heretofore, the people of Europe had known little beyond what the Roman Catholic clergy had taught. For the first time, the Crusaders were exposed to the Eastern World and their minds were broadened. With this new exposure to information and knowledge, the Church's hold on people's minds was weakened and Westerners became open to an expanded learning. It was the discovery of Arabic numerals and the concept of "zero," for example, that made possible both higher mathematics and the ensuing progress in Western science and technology. Their convergence with Eastern religion also affected the spiritual perception of these Western Christians.

The Knights learned that the Infidels had a higher code of honor than they themselves did and often lived up to it better. Somewhere along the line, their cavalier warlike spirit and craving for adventure reached upward into a new code of ethics and behavior. This new code was a compelling force in the birth of the Age of Chivalry and an entirely new culture concerned with the quality of human life: The Renaissance, the great intellectual affirmation of the human spirit.

The Knights assembled into religious and mystical Orders to champion the principles of truth and right. They vowed to use their strength to defend against injustice and evil and to protect women, children, the feeble and defenseless. Those were violent times in which it was customary to give no quarter. It is extraordinary that those kinds of consideration and treatment would have been bestowed on anyone in those days. Yet the Knights extended their code to everyone. They were pledged to give generously to all who were in need.

This new elevation of Knighthood required a highly rigorous educational system. Exceptional young boys entered as candidates for Knighthood at age seven. Throughout their long training they underwent many tests to prove their worthiness. As they grew older and stronger, their trials became increasingly severe. These sacred ordeals were called "Initiations." Their education was supervised, not by the Church, but by the Lords and Ladies of the Court. In their early years, under the Ladies, they learned manners, religion, reading, writing and music. Later the Lords taught them horsemanship, use of arms, and physical combat and fitness. It is meaningful that the aim of their education was primarily to prepare them for a life here on earth rather than for an ''afterlife.''

Some Knights were also educated in the secret teaching of the Mysteries, and their Orders became powerful organizations to protect and perpetuate the Ancient Wisdom. The Knights of the Golden Stone, for instance, ''Ascribed their Order only to God and His handmaid, Nature.'' As ''Spiritual Warriors,'' they championed Spiritual Truth by humbly serving earthly causes. Knights were obliged never to use their knowledge or power for the attainment of worldly dignity. Once The Spirit found an opening, It continued to develop the knightly resolve that right should prevail and found fascinating ways to persist and live on.

Chivalry, as the Knight's code of honor for the highest kind of service on earth, has captured the imagination of the world ever since. The legends of ''Knights in Shining Armour'' rescuing ''Fair Maidens'' and ''slaying dragons'' became a favorite theme of medieval literature and a permanent part of the human dream for a higher way to live. We can see that admiration for merciful pursuits became ingrained in European languages and customs. In Latin, ''mercis'' means ''reward.'' In French, ''merci'' means ''thanks.'' A standard reply of gratitude for beggars during the Middle Ages was: ''May God reward you in heaven.''

The Grail and the Cup of Cold Water

One of the greatest Western legacies for understanding the true teachings of Jesus and the Inner Christ is contained in the rich symbology of the Legends of King Arthur and the Knights of the Round Table. One legend in particular can be especially illuminating in showing us how the virtues connected with Knighthood and mercy can best be adopted into our modern lives. It involves a Knight in his search for the Holy Grail. As the Knight left the city for his long and dangerous quest, a beggar at the gate asked for alms. The Knight, attentive to his mission, scarcely noticed him and passed him by. Months later the Knight returned from an unsuccessful search, weary and ragged. He encountered the same beggar at the gate and, with resignation, tossed him his last coin. In that instant, the beggar turned into the Christ. This might easily bring to mind Jesus' parable of the Good Samaritan and his merciful act to a stranger.

Mercy is primarily a quality of the inner life. God's mercy, being a gracious disposition towards us with a readiness to forgive, strengthen, inspire and bless, is expressed through us as the same disposition extended towards ourselves and others. To be "merciful" is to live out the inner qualities of tolerance, understanding, forgiveness, love, kindness and all the other spiritually generated attributes that constitute the Christ Character. It is the Divine way of living in the world with a mind and heart bent towards the good. Nothing can bring us closer to being our "Brother's keeper," or unite us in brotherhood than mercy.

Yet, the adage that "charity begins at home" is a sound metaphysical principle. We cannot give what we do not possess. Establishing mercy first within our own lives, especially for our own shortcomings, is the gateway to expressing mercy to the world.

When we seek to achieve a merciful disposition, we soon encounter the necessity of forgiveness ("To give love for"). A merciful attitude is forgiving. Sometimes by giving to charities and "worthy causes" in an ostensible way, we try to camouflage (from ourselves) an inward disposition that has not yet achieved the qualities that truly reflect mercy to others, or earned the right to embody its spiritual benefits for ourselves. But Jesus, in the Sermon on the Mount's treatment concerning giving alms "In secret," tells us that God is not mocked.

Mercy faces its hardest task in us by overcoming our being small in the privacy of ourselves. When we weaken the hold of resentment, jealousy, and prejudice and refuse to nurse them by becoming truly forgiving, our inner power for expressing mercy (first within and then without) will never be stronger. The Good Samaritan will be remembered until the end of time, not because he was a wealthy and generous giver of money, or a great physician, but because his motivation incorporated the qualities of forgiveness and mercy that he could not withhold. He possessed the inner capacity for a Christlike response to a fellow human in need.

The symbology of the Holy Grail can speak to us on many levels as we undergo the preparation and transformational process involved in our quest for Spiritual Truth. Understanding many of the themes found in the Arthurian Legends, however, requires our own conscious awakening to the Truth of our Being, our eternal spiritual identity as Children of God. For example, the search for the Chalice of Eternal Life represents the inner quest for our Higher Self, in which we must be open to who we really are, why we are truly here, and what we can ultimately be. When we drink from That Cup, the Eternal Aspects of our Being (Christ) come alive from the hidden Spring of God's Everlasting Spirit abiding deep within us. They live on through each act of mercy. They flow into every "cup of cold water" (Matthew 10:42).

Candidates for Knighthood

Jesus' fifth Beatitude about mercy is an entreaty for training and testing our own thoughts and feelings as Candidates for Spiritual Knighthood. In order to "walk in another's moccasins" and enter into another's mind and heart, we first must grow beyond the restraints of our own inner impairments. In recognizing our own need for mercy and forgiveness, we should first direct our merciful efforts towards the spiritually deprived concepts and emotions that are always "begging" our attention and care within our own consciousness. In a zealous quest for the Divine Life, the inclination is to seek outwardly for "sacred causes."

As with all spiritual disciplines, the practice of mercy and forgiveness starts with ourselves. To love and honor another, we must first learn to love and honor ourselves. It is by first clearing out the inner negativity, "slaying the dragons" of our own false concepts, seeking out the best that is in us and "rescuing the fair maidens" of our own pure and virtuous emotions that our true and essential nature appears. By working in and on our inner life we can courageously face and overcome our hidden blindness and challenge the fear-based inclinations and illusions that keep us consciously separated from God and each other. In so doing, we can then begin living out the highest ideals that we can understand and apply in our lives. We also become shining emissaries of God's mercy.

In having balanced the spiritual qualities of our inner life with corresponding achievements in our outer life, we become open channels through which God can bestow mercy to all who are in need. In this highly meritorious and praiseworthy human attainment, we pass our midterm examinations as followers of Jesus in "The Way, the Truth and the Life." We have also earned the right to the higher life that can be attained only from a nobly maintained inner life that reflects some of the Character of Christ in gallant and valuable service to "The Fatherhood of God and the Brotherhood of Man."

Angels of Mercy

Yet, Jesus' promise of the blessing of mercy do not end when we reach the limits of our human efforts. Another blessed avenue is available, the reciprocal of earning the right to the blessings of mercy by our own disciplined training and testing of merciful qualities in our consciousness. It comes through Grace, the loving gift of God's Angels of Mercy.

Angels are often considered the celestial helpmates and benefactors fantasized for children's prayers:
Angel of God, my guardian dear,
To whom his love entrusts me here,
Ever this day be at my side,
To light and guard, to rule and guide.

If we were ever aware of them, we often forgot or outgrew our belief in personal guardian angels. But Scripture is loaded with references to angels. There are legions of angels appearing in the Bible from Genesis to Revelation. According to many religions, angels are spiritual beings created by God to act as servants, envoys and messengers between Heaven and earth. The word angel comes from the Greek word "angelos," meaning "messenger."

The Angelic Host has a spiritual kinship with human beings. Its main purpose is to bridge the gap between God and the human race. Angels are traditionally pictured as having a human form with wings, symbolizing their office as sacred intermediaries between the Divine and the human. The wings and halo also represent illumination - the special amplitude of radiance by which ministering angels can meet each person at the exact level of their struggles, difficulties and spiritual discipline to help and guide them towards further spiritual attainment.

There are ranks and echelons in the Angelic Hierarchy. Their devotion to serving the human race takes many forms. Their functions are many. In the vision of Jacob's Ladder, for example, angels ascended and descended between heaven and earth. In the New Testament, it was an angel who announced the coming of Jesus and angels attended Him all through His life. There were angels in charge of the Seven Churches in the Book of Revelation. Angels serve as guardians to entire nations. There are angels of peace, harmony, enlightenment, healing, protection, adjustment, transmutation, nature and so forth.

Metaphysically, angels can be represented in spiritual thought. Because it is not an angelic function to judge or accuse, no matter what the fault, state or condition of our consciousness, angelic messages are always free of ego-obstructions and beyond present human comprehension. Angels have instant access to the knowledge of God and their messenger thought-forms, which come directly through inspiration and intuition, transcend all the encumbrances of lower consciousness. The spiritual wisdom of their lofty thoughts and angelic ideas provides immediate assistance and also develops an enduring higher consciousness. Angelic messages are always "Good tidings of great joy."

Behind the conventional effigy of "fallen angels" is the disclosure of a common transgression that actually occurs within ourselves: the deceptive and vainglorious distortions and adulterations that can befall intuitive, angelic Revelation (immaculatively conceived "Messages from God") by our misguided and delusionary misuse of free-willed choice. It is our function to invite the angelic influences of inspiration, guardianship, mercy, order and harmony into our minds and hearts and then unconditionally accept their higher vision into our concepts and beliefs without any degradation on the part of our own lower consciousness. Then, by Divine Law, through entertaining pure angelic thoughts inwardly, we are assured of experiencing their godly manifestation outwardly.

When involved with the Angels of Mercy, the best guide

is to always err on the side of love. We cannot humanly know, in ourselves or others, all the causes and ramifications that enter into a particular condition or episode that requires mercy. But the Angels do!

We must learn to trust the transcendent visions that inspiration can bring. The Angels can connect us to our Higher Self, the Spiritual part of us that can always behold in each person the Divine Image which God always sees and relates to within each of us. Once we are in touch with our God-Self, the message of each consideration of mercy will be from the Christ, "Inasmuch as ye have done it unto one of the least of these my brethren, ye have done it to me" (Matthew 25:40). When we are connected to the Christ in us, the clear instructions will be to express and become more identified with that same Christ Nature.

The most important Angel for you to believe in - and work closest with - is that wonderful Angel of your own Higher Being (in Abraham Lincoln's words, "The Angels of Our Better Nature") available in the upper reaches of your consciousness. This built-in angelic bridge between a mundane understanding of life and an angelic interpretation from the spiritual point of view can immediately take us into the higher dimension of possibilities of letting the Christ within express the divine nature in our human lives. In a very real sense and in that instant of higher awareness, we are "deputized" as God's Angel for whatever needs to be done to serve God's purposes at that time and place.

"Angels Unawares"

Jesus' Beatitude about mercy is an invitation to seize every moment of spiritual awareness that comes to us and to live it out as God's Knights and Angels of mercy in action. The Apostle Paul tells us that in the exemplary tradition of the Good Samaritan, when we show love to strangers, we might well be "Entertaining angels unawares" (Hebrews 13:2). Shakespeare venerated mercy as an attribute of God enthroned in a human heart. And he wrote:
> "The quality of mercy is not strain'd;
> It droppeth as the gentle rain from heaven
> Upon the place beneath: it is twice blest;

It blesseth him that gives and him that takes.''
At the heart of this Beautiful Attitude is God's Covenant that no matter how much mercy we bestow, we will always receive more than we give: ''Blessed are the merciful, for they shall obtain mercy.''

Chapter Seven

A Noble Heart

"Blessed are the pure in heart: for they shall see God."
This is the most winsome of Jesus' Beautiful Attitudes. It is
easy to see why.

First, it begins with a universally appealing possibility
for any human being who has been involved at all in the common
mistakes, challenges and difficult circumstances that go along
with the normal experiences of living. It proposes the heartening prospect of an inner cleansing and soul-level purification.
The world-encumbered heart longs to be unburdened through
an inner release and regenerated with a sweeping, new spiritual
lease on life.

Next is a promise that answers an even deeper longing of
the human heart. It speaks of the possibility of actually
perceiving God. This added prospect leads to one of the most
exalted and memorable of all human experiences. It fulfills the
desire of every sincere Seeker to authenticate and witness the
Reality of God: Divinity exists! Initially, this quest inevitab-
ly takes on tangible and external pursuits. Even after three
years of personally beholding Jesus' Individualized Disclosures
of God's Indwelling Spiritual Nature through His life and
actions, Philip still voiced the Disciples' singular, exoteric
appeal, "Lord, shew us the Father, and it sufficeth us" (John
14:8). This cry is as old as humanity. It has been a basic
mandate for every religion. Yet, its true realization begins only
with the advent of spiritual vision.

Third, as we develop an understanding of what it really
means to "see God" we will awaken to the spiritual significance
of what our latent capacity just to attain the vision that can
perceive God's Presence in our lives actually attests about us.
We will appreciate the very possibility as a mark of our Divinity.
For those who have "eyes which see," this assurance becomes
an emblem of dignity and greatness for humanity. Jesus brought

a new vision to the world. Within it, He sometimes incorporated spiritual gems and threads of wisdom from the past. In this Beatitude, He reinstated the Old Testament avowal of our Divine Potential, "What is man, that thou are mindful of him? and the son of man, that thou visitest him? For thou hast made him a little lower than God, and hast crowned him with glory and honour" (Psalms 8:4,5 ASV).

Our Many Concepts of God

What is involved, even as a measure of our own True Nature, is our conception of God. For centuries, our image of God has been preponderantly anthropomorphic. God walked and talked and looked like a man. It has been quipped, "God originally created man in His image, and man has been bent on returning the compliment ever since." Our most lingering concept of God was modeled after the prototype of an ancient Oriental Potentate. He was an old man with a white beard who sat on a throne, looked on us askance and ruled with a foreboding predisposition toward jealousy, judgement and punishment. From this masculine-autocratic metaphor, we have brought forward out of antiquity the so-called "God-fearing" relationship that had been founded on the primal concept of a distant, disapproving, often angry God.

This prevailing conception of God gradually softened within Judaism to a somewhat more benevolent relationship for themselves - providing they, in their national identity, faithfully and fully honored the Covenant. But, the notion of God's masculinity never waned. And the strong influence of the presumption of a masculine God has persisted not only in much of our religion, but in our language and customs. For most people, any reference to God, the Eternal, Transcendent Being - in, above and behind all creation - is still in the pronouns "He," "Him," or "His."

Artists have contributed toward this personification with vivid renderings of the God as a man. Once an art teacher, glancing at a young student busily at work on a portrait of a man, asked who he was drawing. He answered, "God." She said, "No one knows what God looks like." He responded, "They will in a few minutes." Even modern moviemakers cast God in a masculine, human role. It is encouraging to note, though, that

even in the older film classic, "Green Pastures," God's disposition has been upgraded to "long suffering"; and more recently, in the person of George Burns, the characterization of
God is warm and delightful. Jesus elevated the entire concept
of God into a spiritual perspective when He said, "Not that any
man hath seen the Father, save he that is from God, he hath seen
the Father" (John 6:46).

Purification

In this Beautiful Attitude, Jesus introduced the possibility of an entirely new relationship with God, one based on
purity, rather than fear. The concern for purity was far from
new to Israelite religious thinking, especially among the priesthood. Through their elaborate codes of purification, every
person as well as every thing in life was precisely classified as
either pure and holy, or unclean and profane. Especially from
the time of Ezra, there were numerous rules, ceremonies and
rituals imposing rigorous mandates for purity and safeguards
against all manners of exterior defilement. For the most part,
they were external requirements and prohibitions pertaining to
food, clothing, marriage, birth, death, sacrifices, and nearly
every activity in the daily life of a Hebrew. Many of these rites
were warranted for protection against disease and, most important to them, against the weakening of the Hebrew Nation and
their religious tradition.

There was also awareness among the ancient Hebrew
sages of the importance of inward purification underlying all the
external observances. The Psalmist, especially, had recognized
that the "experience" of God was usually the privilege of "He
that hath clean hands, and a pure heart" (Psalms 24:4).

Jesus' great emphasis, however, was solely on the need
for purification in the hidden recesses of our inner lives; not on
legalistic compliance with outer practices. In order to reverse
the thinking and redirect attention inward, He found it necessary to severely criticize the overriding emphasis of the priesthood on the outwardly oriented purification rites. He also
denounced the Pharisaic interests in external purity as hypo-
critical and misleading. To Jesus, the pathway of purification
is from within.

Consistent with His Pronouncement that "The Kingdom of God is within you" is His representation of purity as an inward, intimate, often private matter between each individual and God. Jesus summarized His whole teaching on purity in this Beatitude. And, again, He reintegrated into His teachings some of the extraordinarily poetic insights of the Psalmist:

"Behold, thou desirest truth in the inward parts; and in the hidden part thou wilt make me to know wisdom. Purify me with hyssop, and I shall be clean: wash me, and I will be whiter than snow. Make me to hear joy and gladness, That the bones which have broken may rejoice. Hide thy face from my sins, and blot out all mine iniquities. Create in me a clean heart, O God; And renew a right spirit in me" (Psalms 51:6-10).

This concept has never been easy to incorporate into orthodox religious practices, however. Even the Disciples, themselves, had a major problem involving purity in accepting the early non-Jewish Christian converts. Baptism quickly became a religious recruiting implement. To this day, there are those who insist that Eternal Salvation depends exclusively on some particular observance of the external application of water.

Baptism

In my own attempt to arrive at the spiritual significance of Baptism as a symbol for inner purification, I began by recalling from my youth the distinct discomfort of working on a threshing crew in the wheat harvest. It surely was one of the dirtiest jobs in the world. By the end of a very long day, the accumulated incrustation of dust and wheat chaff felt as though I were wearing long underwear made out of "hair shirt." The unbridled relief of finally being able to dive headlong into an irrigation ditch and let the dirt and grime wash away was true bliss.

Years later, I stood on the banks of the river Jordan. I had just visited Qumran, the ancient site of the monastic order of the Essenes. Their emphasis on ceremonial washing necessitated hand-carrying gallons of water up a steep desert trail in order to maintain pools for daily baths. It is possible that John the Baptist was affected by, or even affiliated with, Essenism. With this in mind, I began to imagine what living in the desert might have been like for many of our biblical ancestors. I had heard that many of them had only a few precious baths in their whole lives. It was easy for me to relate to the exuberance and even ecstasy involved if they were ever able to arrive at the River Jordan, jump in and wash away months, even years, of dirt!

From there, I could further imagine someone in the exaltation of their freshly acquired bodily cleanliness reflecting how wonderful it would be if only there were a way to also be made as clean inside. Perhaps, this is how the ritual of Baptism began. The refreshment and exhilaration of submerging oneself in moving water is a profound and vibrant symbol for experiencing the total immersion of the inner life in the cleansing, purifying and renewing activity of spiritualized consciousness. Certainly, from the account of His Spiritual Baptism of the Disciples (sans water) when he appeared to them in the Upper Room (a symbol of Higher Consciousness), Jesus regarded It essentially as a vital inner cleansing process imperative to spiritual maturity and transcendence.

A Clean Heart

"Create in me a clean heart, O God. And renew in me a right Spirit." Only the pure in heart know the fullness of life. As in the second Beatitude, Jesus used the word "heart" to designate all the inner dimensions of our human personality. It includes our stored knowledge, values, feelings, faith, wisdom and accumulated spiritual understanding. It further includes the latent Pattern of Perfection of our True Spiritual Self, the God Image and Likeness in which we were created, no matter how remotely hidden. It ultimately includes the entire inner repository of our spiritual inheritance from God: all that is essentially pure, whole, true and Godlike. Every Quality of Christ lies dormant here.

Our heart is the source of all the internal forces and emotional powers that drive and shape our lives. It is the birthplace of our hopes, dreams, longings and desires. Our heart is God's treasury of Good within us. A pure heart is the fountainhead of a healthy, holy, hallowed life.

In recognizing that the heart is the origin of the ennobling virtues and qualities of consciousness by which we can purely experience and express God, Jesus undoubtedly knew "by heart" the Proverb, "Keep thy heart with all diligence; for out of it flow the issues of life" (Proverbs 4:23). For Jesus, it was also the heart and not the situations, conditions and circumstances in life that was the source of our burdens, troubles and difficulties. "There is nothing from without the man, that entering into him can defile him: but the things which come out of him, those are they that defile the man" (Mark 7:15).

It can be very startling to many people to be told that, in the long run, they cause what happens to them. Yet from the spiritual perspective that we were made in God's Image and given free will, the prevailing conditions and environment in which we find ourselves are not due to chance nearly as much as we believe. Our lives are ultimately determined by our own choices, greatly influenced and colored by our predominant inner attitudes. We may exclaim, "Oh, no!" But it's true.

In the soul curriculum of this earth-life, the basic reason for what we attract into our experiences is that, at some time and some place along the line, we have made the choices that brought it about. Our troubles and frustrations with people and situations are often due to unresolved conflicts and tensions within ourselves. We complain, accuse, make someone else the culprit; but we, primarily, manufacture the cause of most of our troubles and then draw them to ourselves inadvertently, even habitually. Trouble doesn't just happen. In some way, often unconsciously, we get ourselves into a position for it to occur. The most responsible position we can take for our maximum spiritual growth and development is to acknowledge that, as far as our own challenges and difficulties are concerned, we will be answerable for how we react and for the choices we will make from the present moment on.

Jesus pointed out the inescapable relationship between what is in our hearts and what we experience in life. He emphasized that when the heart is not pure, we deprive ourselves of the inner access to the qualities of Reality of our Nature. The word "Christ" shares the same derivation as the word "crystal." Jesus, through the ultimate clear mind and pure heart of His Christ Consciousness, gave crystalline expression to the entire spectrum of God's Nature latent within every human being. In the absolute purity of His expressions of Truth, goodness, understanding, wisdom, forgiveness, compassion and love, Jesus displayed the many possibilities vested in each of us to reflect God's Image in our lives. Then, He unmasked the areas of hidden causes and inner divisions that pollute and block our efforts to express these same Godlike qualities of our own Real Self. Jesus emphasized that when our own heart is not pure, we are spiritually blinded and therefore unaware and unresponsive to the Reality and Divine Possibilities of our True Nature.

Through the Eyes of Christ

The Bible stories about the experiences of Jesus reveal the glorious way that He Expressed God in His Life. As a standard for which we are to aspire in our own thinking, Paul invited our attention to the Christ Mind that He possessed. The sacredness and purity of Jesus' heart has likewise become a beautiful object of adoration and worship. Implied in this Beatitude is also the invitation to think about what Jesus saw in life. He brought a new vision. It can change the way we look at everything.

We miss much of what Jesus saw in life. In the Sermon on the Mount, especially, Jesus placed before us a powerful and creative new way of seeing God, ourselves, and life itself. The vision is spiritual, a crystal-clear vision of Oneness, goodness, love and all that is True and Godlike.

Jesus told us in many different ways that we do not essentially find God in a place, person, book, or anything outside our own mind and heart. His vision of everything was always extended into God's Omnipresence. To Him, the only place in the entire cosmos that the Presence of God could be absent was in the awareness of a human being intellectually blinded by negative illusions and blocked by the emotions of fear, guilt, resentment, and frustration held in our hearts. In correcting our wrong view of life, Jesus recognized that we live largely by how we feel. He gave prime attention to expunging from our emotional nature all that contaminates our vision and prevents us from relating to the world with the purity of a spiritual perception. The special objective of this Beautiful Attitude is in cultivating and refining a consciousness that is capable of spiritual discernment. When we achieve any awareness of God's Presence, we see everything in a different light. It is in the purification of our hearts that our spiritual eyes are opened.

To be pure means to be washed and cleansed. It also means the absence of being mixed or divided. Applied to the process of spiritual development, the purification of our hearts not only removes the deterrents to the inner creative activity that invokes our True Nature, but it also unifies our whole inner life into the unity of purpose that Jesus termed the "single eye." The quality of emotional mastery that He called "pure in heart" involves the integration of all the inner dimensions of our personality into a consciousness of God. A pure heart is centered and poised in Spirit and mobilized into a clear channel for the good only. The pure in heart can discern the Divine Element in everything and everyone, and they are capable of finding God anew in every encounter. To the pure in heart, all things are pure. This vision of spiritual purity is a powerful force for good in the world.

The Art of Elimination

The process of purification is basically the art of elimination. The good news is that a little purity goes a long way. We do not have to be "sinless," nor do we need to deny ourselves the right expression of our natural desires. Purity rids us of only that which is false and unnatural. Allowing ourselves to recognize the darkness in any negative emotion can help us to dispel it. When accepted or invited into a receptive consciousness, the Light of Truth can transmute any darkness or negativity that has been lodged there. A single revealing spiritual insight can change the course of our life.

It is always the pure hearted that "see" God, never the intellectually bright or theologically learned. Rules and rituals can invoke an inner receptiveness to change, but it is Truth that lights our minds and love that creates a pure heart. The Sermon on the Mount emphasizes all the way through that it is the state of our mind and heart that determines what we see and experience in life and produces the world in which we live. The special promise of this Beatitude is that inner purity can produce a great change in our lives. It is effected through a vision that takes us into a new world, a beautiful world in which the inner and outer become one: the grass is greener, the sky is bluer, God is a Living Presence and each human being is a Holy Child of God. A spiritual rebirth and renewal always begins with a vision in which we see what we have not seen before.

Seeing God is not limited to optics. We actually see very little with the physical eye; it is mostly a matter of spiritual awareness. To see God is to realize the Divine Presence in any way, right in the midst of the ups and downs and laughter and tears of our ordinary lives. It is to see the profound in the familiar, the goodness and glory of God shining through the commonplace. It means that wherever we look, we find some evidence of God's Nature in each experience.

Practicing the Presence of God

For centuries, we have been taught to practice the absence of God. Then, a little Monk named Brother Lawrence gave humanity a simple, but wonderful insight when he learned to **Practice the Presence** of God while washing the Monastery dishes. This, the "**Single Eye**" at the center of the Sermon on the Mount (Matthew 6:22), had been the true focus of all that Jesus taught.

To behold life through the purified vision of a devout and noble heart is to experience an ever-increasing intimacy and alliance with the Light of the Divine intelligence, power, order, will and love involved in Creation's supreme work of manifesting God's qualities and attributes in every nook and cranny of life. It also engenders an inestimable sense of wonder, gratitude, beauty and appreciation. Blessed indeed are the "pure in heart."

Chapter Eight

Shalom

"Blessed are the peacemakers: for they shall be called sons of God"!

War is the dominate curse of the human race. Strangely enough, many wars have been fought with some of the most noble idealism and pure-hearted sacrifice and courage ever displayed by humanity. All wars establish their foundations in religiosity. Every war becomes a "holy war." Both sides in any war tend to enlist the support of their particular concept of Deity and adopt a spiritual overtone that places them on "God's side" - the side of right (valid even in ideologies of so-called "godless" societies).

In seeking sacred justification and the conformation of spiritual values and noblesse of high purpose in war, we have sometimes borrowed and adapted the preceding Beatitude, "Blessed are the pure in heart: for they shall see God." For 1600 years, Christianity has sanctioned the concept of fighting for "just cause" in war after war: "My eyes have seen the glory of the coming of the Lord...I have seen Him in the watchfires of a hundred circling camps" ("The Battle Hymn of the Republic").

But in regard to war, our hearts are yet confused, our vision still limited. An English Diplomat once proposed this tongue-in-cheek question to Napoleon: "Your majesty, conceding that before a battle each side prays to God for victory, how does God decide who will win?" Napoleon replied: "I can only answer that based on my own experience. God invariably favors the army with the most artillery." And, perhaps this is our greatest tragedy - in war we tend to prepare the most and squander our best for the worst!

It isn't that most people don't want peace. Quite to the contrary, a large majority of the citizens of this planet are tired and weary of hostility and opposed to war. Ironically, most of

our world problems are outgrowths of our endeavors and
maneuvers for peace.   We also try to achieve peace by
defensively ''arming to the teeth'' - the unwitting causative
factor for a new war.   And we have also discovered a double
irony, we can win a war and lose the peace.   Above all, we seem
to have finally begun to realize that no war will ever end war.

Yet, warfare is not the only way we breach the peace.   A
combat soldier in World War II pleaded in a letter to his nagging
wife, ''Let me fight the war in peace!''   True peace lies beyond
cease-fire.   Even when there is no war, we find that peace is
still that for which the world mostly yearns.

Shalom

The concept of peace, as it was evolved through the
Hebrew word ''Shalom,'' represented one of the earliest ideals
to which our spiritual ancestors aspired and beseeched God.
Deeply rooted as an imperative for survival, it grew to be
considered a prime requirement for a harmonious and agreeable
existence.   ''Shalom'' was incorporated into their formal prayers,
Psalms and Benedictions, as well as their everyday greeting to
friends and strangers alike and - of great significance - into the
name of their beloved Jerusalem (Jeru-shalom), ''The Fortress
of Peace,'' a condition neither It nor the world has ever yet
enjoyed.   The peace which Jesus cherished for all people
elevated the richness of the word Shalom into the ultimate
blessedness of peace.   It fully encompassed the grace of spiritual
security, wholeness and well-being found only in a reconciliation between any human belief in separation from God or each
other and an abiding consciousness of Spiritual Oneness.

Today, after centuries of conflict, the true Peacemaker is
not only much needed in our world, but would be one of the
major benefactors of all time.   It is very easy to feel that peace
will be achieved by diplomats, heads-of-state and a few exceptional personages; it is far more likely to be attained through you
and me.   The causes of all wars have always been the private
wars of individuals, the ''civil wars'' that often rage within each
of us.   The first and most important steps, therefore, are in the
individual.   It is the privilege and responsibility of each of us to
be Peacemakers.

True Peace

What is peace? It is not, as often believed, merely the cessation of conflict and the absence of strife. Peace is an active, powerful, positive creative force in its own right. Peace is an extension of Spiritual Oneness. Perhaps most explicit, true peace is an energized state of freedom from inner discordance into free-flowing expression of the sovereign activity of God. It is a spiritual quality and like all the potential, divine capabilities and attributes which we inherit as Children of God, peace is an activity that must be generated (''made'') from within ourselves. The transition from the old Hebrew idea of peace to the new concept expressed by Jesus hinged on His emphasis on inwardness. He nearly always connected peace with an untroubled mind and a calm, poised and serene heart that is inspired and maintained by a deep sense of spiritual alliance with God.

Peace, as a formative spiritual quality, is really the first step in the expression of all other spiritual qualities. With the I AM Teachings of His Upper Room (Higher Consciousness) ''Farewell Address,'' in turning us over to the Indwelling Spirit of God that It might begin to work in us as It had in Him (''Which is the Holy Spirit'' John 14:26 ASV), He was inviting us to share all the coherent qualities of God that He had revealed in His own life. He was inviting us to share His Nature as the Christ!

He established the dynamics of this entire inner process on peace: ''Peace I leave with you; my peace I give unto you: not as the world giveth, give I unto you. Let not your heart be troubled, neither let it be afraid'' (John 14:27). The peace of Christ, in replacing the inner constraints of fear-based opposition, furnishes a new stabilized platform in our consciousness for launching all the other spiritual and creative activity potential in us.

To elaborate: Do not confuse His peace with victory over the Romans, or any nation, institution, system or form of opposition or confrontation that you find in the world. Nothing in the world can give true peace. No amount of clever negotiation or manipulation of circumstances can bring this peace. Nothing of the world can provide a peace that is not temporary, incomplete or shallow. Peace does not come from without. Peace ("My Peace") comes from the Christ nature - and brings forth the Christ Nature.

The things that are involved in peace are inward and spiritual. How, then, do we bring peace into the world? Through changing ourselves. Peace comes with a new consciousness. The very desire for this is within our True Nature. Albert Schweitzer, the famous missionary-doctor who worked with Africans, was asked how he interested them in the Gospel of Jesus. He replied that he never preached to them about sin, law or any negatives. "I strive to awaken in their hearts a longing peace with God. When I speak to them of the difference between a restless and a peaceful heart, the wildest savage knows what is meant. And when I portray Jesus as 'He who brings peace with God to the hearts of men,' they comprehend Him."

The Peacemaker

Likewise, a true Peacemaker is not an arbiter or referee, nor someone who intrudes or interferes in the affairs of others and attempts to impose peace. Rather, the Peacemaker expresses the qualities from which peace can come.

Peace does need to be "made." It never comes without an endowment on our part. We cannot express a quality that is lacking in us. A "maker" of peace is one who first brings forth peace in his or her own thoughts and feelings and then lets it flow forth into his or her life and world. Outer peace always depends on inner peace. Peacemakers, therefore, must prepare their mind and heart for expressions of peace. They can succeed by creating in their inner life all that is born out of goodwill, harmony, trust and love, and cultivating a positive, God-directed attitude from which their consciousness can become a living fountain of these qualities.

Peace is a form of spiritual awareness. It is born in silence and calmness. When Jesus calmed the winds and sea, just as when He said, "Let not your hearts be troubled, "He was emphasizing the creative power latent in stillness and quietude. God works best through us when we are calm and speaks best to us in ''the still small voice'' (I Kings 19:12). It is in the Silence that God imparts the power of spiritual awareness. In peacefulness and poise we are given the consciousness by which we can become Peacemakers. "And the peace of God, which passeth all understanding, shall keep your hearts and minds through Christ Jesus" (Philippians 4:7).

Deep within, in the stillness of our innermost being abides a Center from which all peace comes. Peace originates here in the quietness of Spirit. The process begins in us by establishing thoughts and feelings of peace which, when nourished, quicken a flow of peace-filled consciousness that can permeate all the multilevels of our personalities and then expand into our outer lives. It is by learning to go into the inner silence, if only for a moment, that we best open the way for peace.

Selah

Another Hebrew word, "Selah," can help provide a gateway into the Peaceful Kingdom within as a prelude to a powerful outward spiritual expression. Selah is a liturgical-musical term, indicating a pause before the grand upliftment of voices in the singing of the Psalms. It contains somewhat the same spiritual meaning as the Sabbath, a returning and resting in the stillness of our inner consciousness, in which we are blessed with hallowedness and infused with spiritual strength. It connotes a creative rest-stop in which we relax our mental and emotional efforts and "Wait on the Lord, and keep his way" (Psalms 37:34). By entering an awareness of God's Abiding Presence in a period of silence, we experience a sense of inner harmony, tranquility, and receptivity through which the Holy Spirit can empower our entire being. "Selah" is a signal to stop and be silent. It can be a wonderful reminder that before beginning any course of attainment or taking any action, we should first pause and retreat into a silent realization of the waiting repository of our God-given potential.

This procedure for drawing on our inner resources is more commonplace than one might suppose. Have you ever observed an athlete preparing himself right before giving his best effort? A baseball pitcher, for example, repeatedly tugs on his cap, licks his fingers, adjusts his pants and kicks at the dirt on the mound. The batter hits his shoe cleats with the bat, spits over his shoulder and so forth. This is "Selah": preparing a state of mind poised for action. All of us tend to take deep breaths to call forth our reserves when presented with a challenge (long ago associated with aspiration: "But there is a spirit in man, and the breath of the Almighty giveth them understanding" Job 32:8 ASV).

One of the excellent reasons to have a ready supply of meaningful affirmations of Spiritual Truth committed to memory is for instant referral when encountering any need to quickly reestablish a serene and stable inner center in consciousness from which to proceed. "In returning and rest shall ye be saved; in quietness and in confidence shall be your strength" (Isaiah 30:15).

A strong inner control can soon be developed by learning to work with "bit-sized-'peaces'." To earn tuition for Ministerial Training, I endured a very tedious job that required a lot of concentration in a noisy and hectic surrounding. The most irksome distraction was the frequent ringing of telephones. One day I decided to attempt to "Agree with thine adversary quickly" (Matthew 5:25). I prepared myself so that each time a phone rang, I would stop whatever I was doing for an instant and use the distraction to remind me that I was still in God's Presence. The effect was amazing. I would quickly find myself once more in a peaceful and positive inner atmosphere.

Later, when I found it difficult to keep my resolve high, I would practice Selah by reciting the entire Twenty-Third Psalm over and over until the words of that beautiful prayer-poem became living expressions of Shalom - an experience of reconciliation and grace. I was learning that one of the most important disciplines of a Peacemaker, as the ancient Psalmist knew, was in establishing a peaceful inner stronghold of God-related awareness to fall back on: "God is our refuge and strength, a very present help in trouble" (Psalms 46:1).

From this experience, I extended the use of the "Selah technique" to a wider range of opportunities to "make" peace. First, though, I needed to learn that any tendency to use affirmations of Spiritual Truth as a way to simply avoid facing problems was as naive as whipcreaming garbage (it comes back through all too soon!). A peacemaker does not ignore problems, but faces them from a spiritual vantage point of transcending thought as a way for reconciliation into a higher level. I like to think that Daniel looked the lion right square in the eye before lifting his face toward God. Part of "making" peace is in recognizing the need for releasing the potential for peace encased in evasive denial and compromise.

From Military to Spiritual Warrior

I am using myself as an example because "peace-making" has played an important role in my commitment to spiritual development. Becoming a Minister did not relieve me of worldly problems. To the contrary, I have had many experiences that have been challenging and "brought my back up." But most of the peace-making has been within myself. Prior to entering the Ministry, I had been a trained warrior, first as a Marine Rifleman and then as an Air Force jet Fighter-Pilot. Aggression and confrontation was the "name of the game."

Needless to say, the opportunities to become a peace-maker have been more than ample. Gradually I learned to recognize that anytime an annoyance, exasperation, frustration or anger in me was covered over with a pretense of peace, I lost access to all that was being blocked by these buried and festering feelings. Ironically, it was in actually "losing my peace" that I was given the insight and determination to make peace in a way that was real and lasting.

Occasionally, to reconcile my feelings about releasing anger, it helped me to remember the honest aggravation that Jesus displayed when He threw the money-changers out of the Temple. My persistence in making inner peace eventually paid good dividends in growth and serenity. Some of the greatest releases I have ever known came when I exercised my Divine Right of free will in choosing peace instead of opposition. I endeavor now to be a "Spiritual Warrior": not one who fights, but who takes a stand for Spiritual Principles and holds to the "Sword of Truth" within.

Prayer and meditation are the master tools of a Peacemaker. It is from the deep prayer of the "Inner chamber" (Matthew 6:6), transcendent to the superficial levels of our humanly controlled consciousness, that we gain the integral unity and creative composure that produce the most effective manifestation of spiritual energy in our lives.   Through prayer we can also greatly amplify our individual influence as "Peacemakers" by linking our peace-inspired consciousness in a creative union with the prayers for peace of people all over the world: "For where two or three are gathered together in my name, there am I **(I AM)** in the midst of them" Matthew 18:20). The power of spiritually heightened collective consciousness is recognized more and more as a significant means for achieving world peace.   This recognition serves as a reminder that true peace does not come from anything external.   "My Peace" comes from Christed Consciousness.   It is an expression of God through the individual.

Sons Of God

     Note well the identity Jesus gave Peacemakers: "For they shall be called **Sons of God**"!   This identification is difficult for most people to claim for themselves.   The uniqueness of the Sonship of God expressed through Jesus has understandably caused most of His followers to reject reference to the possibility of this stature for themselves.   However, this reference had been made before the time of Jesus.   The term "sons of God," for example, was sometimes applied to humans in both the Old and New Testament.   The Apostles John and Paul made important references to the possibilities of our attaining this divinely endowed status, but the idea of Spiritual Sonship has never been developed in the doctrinal "enumeration of Christian privileges."   Instead, the Greek mythological concept of "sons of the gods" as immortal, supernatural beings was adopted, and our own "made in God's Image" identity was categorically overridden.

     Jesus, Himself, gave us many vivid images of our own potential to respond to and share in God's Nature.   It is the climax of this Beatitude that we can, by giving expression to our True Nature, become mature expressers - the very embodiment - of God's Character.   As a Peacemaker, each of us can attain the divinely conferred status of "Son," Junior Partner with God and spiritual benefactor to the world.   We need to place the emphasis where Jesus placed it.   We are each very special creations through which God can be expressed.   Jesus told us that if we believed in God's Spirit in ourselves as He believed in God's Spirit in Him, "the works that I do shall he do also; and greater works than these shall he do'' (John 14:12).

Accordingly, lasting peace is found in giving expression to our Inner Christ Nature, our Divine Self. We need to identify ourselves as Peacemakers. What a beautiful image to have of ourselves! What a wonderful way to conform to the likeness of Christ! I AM a Peacemaker.

Shalom!

Chapter Nine

Hangeth in There!

"Blessed are they that are persecuted" seems a strange finale to the Beatitudes. It probably isn't at all what we would expect from the preceding Beautiful Attitudes that Jesus would have us cultivate in order to evolve into the Kingdom of Higher Life. The anticipated blessing one might ordinarily assume from His mounting Beatitudinal promises is that this would be the place for a "happily ever after" ending.

Up to now, Jesus' Beatitudes have dealt generally with unassailable, inner qualities: the beneficial qualities of character that grow from study, prayer and meditation; spiritual qualities that bring forth the Christ Nature; positive qualities that could conceivably be developed in a monastery or the cave of a hermit. But now we come to the climacteric impact these invisible qualities can bring to everyday living. In this Beatitude, we get a caution: Jesus tells us that when we audaciously apply the Christ Principle in our lives, there not only remain challenges ahead but - at times - they could be exceedingly difficult; even, humanly, menacing. It had been this way for Him and, most likely, would be for us. The reception that someone who follows Christ encounters at the hands of the world is often much less than "Christian."

This is one of the enigmas of the spiritual life. It would seem that a flawless, incomparable life such as that of Jesus would surely evoke boundless veneration and that even the hardest heart would open to Him. But instead, Jesus forewarns us that the world will persecute those qualities of character that grow from the Sermon on the Mount.

A Revolutionary Revision

This concluding Beatitude calls for a revolutionary revision of what we expect to get out of life - and how we expect to get it. All of us, I am sure, have been taught and became accustomed to the notion that if we are "good" we will be rewarded with something good and if - on the other hand - we are "bad," we can expect to be punished. "Reward and punishment" has been the basic indoctrination approach that underlies all our worldly systems of education, motivation and control. It is woven into the pattern of nearly all human development, beginning with early child-raising in the family, school, and religion, and continuing on in the professional, economic, political, social and cultural areas of life. However, as a standard for behavior and a guide for living, this theory is far more negative than positive. It is, essentially, a fear-based approach to life. Fear is the most common, yet most ignoble and inhibiting basis for most of our human endeavors. How apt we are to pride ourselves in our humble "**fear** of God." Yet, in the original Aramaic, the word meant "**awe**" loving respect, the way any beneficent parent would want their children to relate to them. The Apostle Paul shared with Timothy his vision for a much higher, prayer-based approach from which to live: "Wherefore I put thee in remembrance that thou stir up the gift of God, which is in thee through the putting on of my hands. For God hath not given us the spirit of fear; but of power, and of love and a sound mind" (II Timothy 1:6,7).

Jesus' last Beatitude might seem to counter this vision, but His intent was not to induce more fear. He wanted us to understand the pivotal difference between destructive, debasing fear and constructive precaution and discretionary courage. He was telling us that we live in a world in which high virtues and uprightness must overcome resistance. Although He didn't mean that the opposition would be lasting, it will be there, and we should be prepared for it. "Behold, I send you forth as sheep in the midst of wolves: be ye therefore wise as serpents, and harmless as doves" (Matthew 10:16).

In His own life, by the time He gave the Sermon on the Mount, Jesus had found that His own people had responded to Him with an antagonistic and life-endangering opposition that led to the Cross. He was bracing His Disciples for this opposition. Indeed, it was His followers who would attract the most infamous of all opposition and oppression: The Roman Persecution. Yet, the early Christians were not persecuted simply because the Romans were such atrocious people. Compared to other strong nations in history, they were fairly civilized and reasonable. Their main requirement for the conquered people they ruled was that their Roman laws and orders be strictly obeyed. Punishment was quick and harsh, it's true. They nailed rebels to crosses and occasionally threw dissenters to the lions, but how much worse is that than bombs and napalm?

The disquieting element in the teachings of Jesus was that they went beyond "reward and punishment," "law and order" and any of the ordinary ways we have learned to live. He presented an entirely different criteria for life - a new way of thinking with higher values and standards and an emphasis on love and spiritual rightness that the Romans knew nothing about. This drastically challenged the status quo, not only of the Roman Empire, but of all the world. Radical change was inherent in Jesus' Message and inevitable in the life of anyone who would accept and apply It. At the heart of the Truth in which He reveals a higher meaning and purpose to living is the revelation that life, itself, is essentially a spiritual evolution. Only by seeing our everyday experiences in this light can we appreciate them as part of a grand lesson by which we are refined and sensitized to higher, finer influences and evolve upward and onward in our spiritual development.

The Challenge in Change

Yet, without a prodding, often rousing "boot in the pants" from Spirit, human nature changes very reluctantly. Even when we occasionally invite change, it often seems to come a little before we feel we are ready for it. Actually, most innovative ideas represent a challenge to the status quo and a rejoinder to our present system. The tyrant, especially, cannot cope with new ideas or tolerate change. Tyranny can be found on all levels of life. It exists in government all the way down through politics, finance, business, unions, education, religion, neighborhoods and families and - often overlooked but exceedingly important - the intimidation and oppression within ourselves of all new concepts by our emotionally entrenched bastion of dogmatic beliefs and prejudices. We find so many rationalizations and justifications for keeping things the way they are and rarely realize how much these block us from our highest good. Oscar Wilde, for example, saw through it: "The longer I live, the more keenly I feel that whatever was good enough for our fathers is not good enough for us."

God is constantly involved in changing our world for the

better, most desirably when we accept it and cooperate. But, much of the time we resist the change and cling to the security of the familiar world which the innovation seems to threaten. For the most part, we are so apprehensive about anything that alters the conditions we are used to that we become blind to the great potential we have for evolution towards Christhood. Our stubborn defense against new ideas and the changes they represent tends to prevent our chances to grow and imprisons us in our present level of awareness.

The Romans waged their persecutions against the Christians for the same reason that we resist new ideas in our lives - uninvited change. That era represents a classic example of the conflict between the dynamic impetus to move forward and upward in life and the strenuous and tenacious resistance that is involved in all human change. The Roman Persecutions became a dreadful race of whether Rome could kill the Christians off faster than they could win new converts. The Christians won. Their dauntless convictions and magnificent courage, the sheer vitality and splendor of their spiritually transformed lives constituted a power so different and great that a new world would eventually need to be provided for it. The Romans had the power of politics and worldly might. They had the power to punish, harm, imprison and kill. But gradually they were overcome and eventually converted by the greater power of the followers of the Christ Way, who - as they were being harmed and hurt - in turn, forgave and blessed their persecutors. It was a power that could not ultimately be withstood. It was incarnate evidence of the most powerful force in the world! "Ye are of God, little children, and have overcome them: because greater is he that is in you than he that is in the world" (I John 4:4). The first century Christians were incredible, exciting, and invincible even in death. There has never been a story of spiritual triumph quite like it in the history of the world!

On the surface, it may appear that Jesus is saying to His followers: Go out and get yourself persecuted, because you won't be a real Christian until you do. He didn't mean at all that we were to set out to stir up trouble as a badge of honor. This sort of thing leads to a martyr complex, which is based on self-righteousness and masqueraded self-exaltation. The promotion and glamorization of personality does not pay great or lasting "spiritual dividends" (as unmasked in the Second Temptation).

Jesus wasn't saying that, in itself, suffering is ever blessed. What Jesus was stressing was that genuine, animated goodness - that which is higher in any form - does provoke opposition from that which is lower. Yet, the blessing emerges when, through our spiritual commitment, we use the very hardships and sufferings of persecution as opportunities to rise as spiritual victors; and, as He proved on the Cross, also lift others along with us. "And I, if I be lifted up from the earth will draw all men unto me" (John 12:32). This is a triumph in righteousness for the goodness of God. And when we are part of it, we are in the company of the greatness of all the spiritual overcomers of history.

Torchlighters and Trailblazers

Many Bible characters triumphed over persecution and lifted the entire human race to new levels. Abraham, Jacob, Joseph, Moses, the Classic Prophets, the Disciples and Paul (who began as a persecutor of Christians and then seemed to charge headfirst into every conceivable kind of persecution himself as a Christian) are all good examples.

Numerous torchlighters and trailblazers since have then been persecuted for new ideas. Dr. Ignaz Semmelweis, who fought for sterilization and clean hands in medicine, was driven mad by the persecution of his fellow doctors. Florence Nightingale was slandered, hissed, misrepresented and opposed bitterly when she tried to get decent nursing care for wounded soldiers.

Few people realize how much the Founding Fathers of the United States of America were individually persecuted for their roles in the nation's establishment. They had shown deep spiritual responsibility in brilliantly conceiving a highly inspired form of government with freedom to change and grow built into its heart and soul. These illumined and courageous gentlemen most definitely belong to the revered class of Overcomers that Jesus referred to in this Beatitude. The unique gift from the Founding Fathers of America to all humanity was a vision that changed the course of history. Their particular genius came from an inspired, mystical insight. They foresaw the spiritual destiny of the democratic nation they were conceiving and they believed that the birth of the United States was the most important event since the birth of Christ.

The Constitution embodies a new Divine Model of government - a nation truly "Under God" which recognized the Truth of God's Presence within every person as "Self-evident" - destined to help lead all humanity out of bondage and lift every individual into the spiritual realization of the Divine Promise of their being.

The American Founding Fathers openly concealed the spiritual symbology of their vision in The Great Seal of the United States found on every U.S. dollar bill. This design features one of the world's oldest and most durable emblems proclaiming the divine nature and spiritual destiny of humanity: the Mystical Pyramid with "The stone the builders rejected," "The All-seeing Eye of God" and below, the words "Novus Ordo Seclorum," "A New Order of the Ages" ("New Age"). They were the first to recognize the risk and resistance from the Old World order of mentality in such a quantum change. To affirm their faith in the victorious overcoming spirit within humanity, they also incorporated the **American Eagle** into the complementary face of The Great Seal.

Important changes preparing for the advent and break-through of the worldwide "consciousness revolution" have long been underway, usually seed-small and unrecognized for their significance. Much more apparent has been the corollary persecution that has continued into the present, most heinously with such outstanding examples as the assassinations of Abraham Lincoln, Gandhi, John and Robert Kennedy and Martin Luther King. Yet, the consequences of their actions and commitments have actually made them greater in death than in life and have given us encouraging evidence of the mounting support in the minds and hearts of people for the triumph of the Divine Will for good.

Religious Resistance

In America, there is no longer the danger of the "midnight knock" and being imprisoned or put to death for religious beliefs. Still, there remains much to surmount. Any group that advances a new and higher vision invariably meets tremendous resistance in all of its modes of intolerance, animosity, derisive misrepresentation, character slander and political, economic and social reprisal.

Today, most forms of persecution are less corporal and often more camouflaged and sophisticated. Yet widespread intolerance continues against anyone who tends to be different, right down to the "new kid on the block." This behavior still can contain as much malice and require as much courage - and hold as much promise of a blessed overcoming - as any of the foregoing forms of harassment.

There can be immense loneliness in being involved in any new persuasion, especially religious. Often, it initially takes the strongest resolve to withstand, from within ourselves, the dread of rejection and estrangement rising from our human ego-personalities need to belong; and, therefore, please others. We strive to be accepted and approved of through conforming to tradition. Perhaps this is why, odd as it might seem, those with the most ardent and bellicose bent for persecuting new religious sects are usually those very denominations that most recently met similar animosity when they first emerged under their fledgling "cult" status. It does seem very disappointing, after the valiant stand and triumph of the First Century Christians against their persecution, that any Christians would ever, themselves, become persecutors. Yet, the history of Christianity has been saddened by instance after instance of mass persecutions.

In the present accelerated, breathtaking world changes, religious reactionaries appear increasingly unbridled and resistant to any but their own views. Persecution by those entrenched in "fundamentalism" seems more adamant and contentious than ever in opposing other views.

The use of the term "Fundamentalism," to describe Christian foundational spiritual truth, is a serious misnomer. It is, rather, a recent 20th century adjunct movement within Protestantism. It began as a counteraction to the Post-Reformation "form-criticism" research by modern scholarship into the multiple sources and styles of literature based on free inquiry into the differing layers of historical cultures, traditions and points of view through which the Bible compilation gradually evolved.

The superimposed foundation for Fundamentalist faith became the fierce emphasis of their literal Western "Fear of God" interpretation of the Bible as infallible; arresting all Truth to the premise that God has spoken once and unerringly for all time in their insular, often morose renderings from the King's English of the 17th Century A.D. The assumed authority domination is their self-appointed enforcement of exacting and unrelenting adherence to such beliefs through straightjacket control of everything people think, read, hear or participate in. All noncompliance and disobedience is persecuted with "satanic" labeling and retributive threats of "eternal punishment." "Unbelievers" are held in contempt, condemned and despised. One of the most reprehensible epithets in the doctrinal armory of scorn and reproach is "heretic": "one who thinks for himself." Yet, this very option is the most crucial of all the divinely endowed capacities. The gift of freedom of thought and choice that God has entrusted to every individual is sacred. Free willed choice is the fundamental means that God provided each of us for our soul development and spiritual advancement.

The tenuous and equivocal support for religious Fundamentalism, upheld solely by their own assailant resistance, has been likened to a "hot-air balloon" theory that, if anything can ever prick even one factual hole in its external fabric, the whole postulate will come down. This anchors all professions of faith to a spiritually debasing negative-defense-posture. God, Christ and Spiritual Truth **never** need our paltry defense. Only human ego with its vested interests requires that.

The Irrepressible Spirit of Truth

But, as we shall see, this antithetic opposition is wondrously anticipated and incorporated right into the Transformational Process by which the Universal Creative Spirit advances all things toward a Higher Good: "Blessed are ye, when men shall revile you, and persecute you, and shall say all manner of evil against you falsely, for my sake" (Matthew 5:11).

The fundamental truth of our existence - as revealed by Jesus - is that God and humanity are Parent and Child. He based all His Teachings on this "Love of God" Principle of the altogether good, loving and perfect Nature of God and the complementary, "Only Begotten" spiritual perfectibility of each of God's beloved Offspring ("Be ye therefore perfect as your Father which is in heaven is perfect" Matthew 5:48).

As we restore and embrace this fundamental relationship of the Family of God in our minds and hearts, we will awaken - from our inherent spiritual perfection as Children of God - all the creative possibilities needed to break through and overcome the self-imposed limitation and alienation that keeps us in human bondage. First, we need to remember the admonition: "For, if you love them which love you, what reward have ye? do not even the publicans the same?" (Matthew 5:46). Then the summons: "Beloved, let us love one another: for love is of God; and every one that loveth is born of God, and knoweth God. He that loveth not knoweth not God; for God is love" (I John 4:7,8). From these two Scriptures, we can base our lives squarely on the unifying Principle of the "Fatherhood of God and Brotherhood of man." We will then be truly ready to bring forth the Golden New Era of Spiritual Transformation promised by the Heavenly Host to the humble shepherds at the time of Jesus' Birth: "Glory to God in the highest, and on earth peace, good will toward men."

That enormous and miraculous change in the world order is now well underway. It is becoming increasingly apparent that the great turning point into a new, higher order of divinely inspired living is coming through surprisingly unlikely and seemingly ordinary, secular individuals - such as a Polish labor leader and a Russian physicist. Both Nobel Peace Prize Holders Lech Walesa and Andrei Sakharov, modern prophets as well as world leaders endured the persecution of prison, abuse and defamation for their prophetic vision of change. Their vision led to an astounding democratic transformation for most of the world and served to invalidate the anticipated catastrophic prophecy of doomsday religion.

Strangely, but not surprisingly, the very idea of "Novus Ordo Seclorum" - the Indwelling Spirit affirming "New Age" - and its Born-From-Above higher individual, national and global manifestation of peace, truth and love (admittedly somewhat tainted by peripheral exploitation) is disavowed, depreci-

ated and persecuted by those who presume to officially eluci-
date, often with blasphemous negativity, all prophecy for the
spiritual fulfillment of the Universal Creator's Supreme Plan of
Good. But this opposition neither negates nor thwarts in the
slightest the spiritual activity and power behind this prophesied
human and global transformation.

It isn't that religion, anymore than economics, politics or
any other form of humanly organized agency is inherently
wrong or bad. And, although rarely represented as such,
religious institutions likewise serve humanity as the vox populi:
the "voice of the people." All the religions of the world have
emerged in order to meet the pertinent needs of the many
diverse and developing levels of understanding within humanity. The promise of this Beatitude, "For theirs is the **Kingdom
of Heaven**" (which completes full circle this same promise
from the First Beatitude) by Its very definition (**"High Ex-
panse"**) is attained through the continuing expansion of our
Spiritual Potential through Higher Consciousness.

The difficulty sets in when transformed awareness and
increased understanding create new ranges of possibilities, and
elevate the hierarchical order and quality of needs. Religion,
like government, serves best when it is linked with change and
growth. This, the potential invoked through change yoked to
the glory of growth - the ultimate gift of free-willed choice - is
an outstanding feature of Jesus' teachings. So far, however,
the thrust of most religions, again reflecting a human tendency,
is that we attempt to enforce change and compliance in others
rather than seeking spiritual transformation within ourselves.
If there is an inherent historical tendency in religion, it is to
dogmatize the original inspiration of their Founder with overlays of doctrine that restrict any and all change. Often the
protective "wrapping" tends to eclipse the initial treasure of
Spiritual Truth.

The supreme purpose of life is the unfoldment of our
Spiritual Nature. Religious tenets that are designed to "protect" particular levels of understanding invariably fossilize
their adherents at those mental and spiritual levels. This stifled,
unreceptive state of mind lends itself to the tyrannical spread of
fear, paranoia, superstition, separation and uncompromising
attempts to arrest everyone else at that level. This is the mental

and emotional matrix of the persecutor.

But, **being** persecuted is also a state of mind, an adverse mental and emotional response, which can be amended and transcended. Persecution can challenge and test our own ability to change. It can serve to jostle our soul and arouse our ennobling spiritual resources. Christianity, especially, has always been spiritually strongest when it was persecuted and weakest when it persecuted others. As we noted, we all like to "belong" and feel "accepted" and "in." But we can pay an awful price for this extravagance of glamourized personality gratification. Life becomes very bound, drab and spiritless when freedom's spark is traded for any form of temporal worldly security.

Spiritual Mastery

Therefore, Jesus is imploring us not to be afraid to take a stand for right ideals and principles in our lives. And He doesn't say that He is sorry for us because of the consequences. Instead, He congratulates us and applauds the majestic inner strength and spiritual advantage we will gain. In this crowning Beatitude, as He later proved on the Cross, Jesus reaffirms that the true blessedness of life is not attained in avoiding the difficult interludes in life, nor in being relieved or rescued from them. The blessedness of life is the result of responding from a spiritual center with the power of Spirit and the courage of our convictions and rising triumphant into Higher Life: "Rejoice, and be exceedingly glad: for great is your reward in heaven: for so persecuted they the prophets which were before you" (Matthew 5:12).

There are many leading shoots into the emerging Age of the Spiritualization of humanity, both within and outside the religious community. Rapidly increasing multitudes are awakening to new levels of spiritual understanding and being inspired with the vision, faith, high-spirited motivation and courage to take a stand and live them out. The inevitable persecution, however, will be met and overcome mainly within their own consciousness. The promise of this Beatitude is that it will be infinitely worth whatever it takes to see it through.

In this capstone Beatitude, we are assured that we will be

able to endure - with exaltation and cheerfulness - whatever persecutions and growth pains our spiritual commitment might bring.   In this concluding lesson of His Beatitudes, Jesus reveals to us the true ''reward'' and ultimate blessing of this life: the spiritual mastery and fulfillment found only in serving as a co-partner with God in moving our lives and our world upward into exciting new levels of creative living.

Turning the Other Cheek

The creative and positive way of meeting the persecution of spiritual challenge was given by Jesus when He said, ''And unto him that smiteth thee on the one cheek offer also the other'' (Luke 6:29).   A slap in the face was the ultimate affront in the Hebrew culture, a ''striking'' symbol for all the adversarial assault we meet in life.   The first blow always hurts and often surprises and provokes us.   The ''other cheek,'' nevertheless, is not a literal shift to passive acquiescence inviting more abuse or misuse.   It is the attitudinal alternative to revengeful retaliation: redeemed, reinstated spiritual understanding.   It reactivates all the higher qualities of spiritual awareness in our consciousness.

This Eastern colloquialism conveys an unassailable strategy for applying the great Spiritual Principle of overcoming evil with good.   It encapsulates the invincible Law of Spiritual Over-coming - the real subject of this pinnacle Beatitude. ''Offering also the other'' transcends the tendency to react on the same level and puts us in charge of ourselves from a higher vantage point.   ''Turning the other cheek'' can regenerate a Beautiful Attitude that is Divinely reinforced with wisdom, peace, patience, forgiveness, faith and - most especially love - which endures all things.

Jesus also gave humanity an ultimate display of the nobility and mastery inherent in valiant, nonresistant reliance upon the Principles and Laws of Christhood during the time of His arrest and crucifixion.   It was His unequivocal, personal proof that this one explicit Spiritually-based Corrective can give us immediate ascendancy into Larger Life and - in that instant - make us exceptional.   Inspired by the teachings of Jesus, Mahatma (''Great Soul'') Gandhi, a non-Christian empowered through the personal embodiment of Jesus' spiritual principles, gave the modern world one of history's rarest individual demonstrations of the translation of this Beatitudinal truth into action. His spiritual gallantry bequeathed to humanity a major upward turning point and one of its finest examples of truly following the Christ Principle of Overcoming.

Life, as presented by Jesus (especially in His Sermon on the Mount), is a learning, growing, unfolding progression. The very nature of the support provided for our maximum spiritual growth and development supplies us not only with the opportunities, but also the persistent challenges we need to mobilize, persevere and evolve. In a curious but persistent way that actually compounds the overall potential benefits of our aptitude for earth-life accomplishments, there is also an inclination on the part of our unredeemed human nature to provide the important creative antithesis within the transformational process. This unique contribution of "negativity" to the outworking of a "higher good" is paradoxically implemented by the stubborn response in which the old and established tends to resist anything new and different and the lower consciousness almost invariably defends and fights against the higher.

Dramatic Confirmation

A landmark confirmation of the rarely recognized role of the antithesis-opposition in the transformational process was again demonstrated in the astounding failed August 1991 coup d'etat by the Soviet right-wing political hard-liners. Following the unforeseen November 1989 demolishment of the world-dividing Berlin Wall, this uprising turned contemporary history on its head while television brought these events before our very eyes. This globally frightening three-day crisis miraculously united an entire defenseless populace into a mammoth rally for freedom and self-determination. This movement energized a groundswell of heroism in "uncommon" common people that successfully stood up to the seemingly undefeatable military might of the old order of despotism. With breathtaking speed, in which it was said that the "Winds of history reached hurricane force," the triumph of the forces of the human spirit over this alarming attempt to reimpose totalitarian dictatorship launched a quantum leap forward. This remarkable synthesizing event was truly a turning point victory for all people - an incredible breakthrough for human advancement. Most amazing of all was the nonviolent method in which the New Revolution was accomplished. This Moment of Truth, described by some participants as a "spiritual purification" and being "born again," was accomplished without arms or bloodshed. Jesus' Principle involving the self-defeat of evil really worked - for all the world to see. (Note in Chapter Eleven the extraordinary coincidence of the three days of the coup and the scriptural symbology of the number "3".)

Every bit as unanticipated was the momentous event of the almost inconceivable August 1993 Israeli-Palestinian Peace Agreement. Once more as the world watched in awe, breathless and astonished, an invisible wall of almost 4000 years of animosity and strife in the land of the Bible began to tumble with a simple "handshake for history." President Clinton pronounced this peace accord as a "great occasion of history and hope...an extraordinary act in one of history's defining dramas."

Incredible changes are taking place in the world. One of the concluding miracles of the 20th Century for freedom, justice and human dignity centers around the historic all-race election that resurrected South Africa from the tomb of the colonial past. Again, more fundamental changes were attained with a handshake than by any army. Each of these four unprecedented events stirred the world with fresh hope and promise and helped begin to build a bridge to a new era in humanity's spiritual progression towards global peace, harmony and coexistence.

It was within this characteristics and dramatic backdrop of human experience that Jesus concluded His Beatitudes with the final, dramatic promise of the inevitable victory of the Christ Way. With Grace, the higher works through and absolves the lower. And in this, He is absolutely assuring us that any new and higher way that is introduced and sustained by Spiritual Consciousness will ultimately always prevail - in a glorious and triumphal reign of God's Good.

Most of the spiritual victories in our personal lives encounter some kind of persecution for "righteousness sake." These challenges and conquests by which we rise to the spiritual heights of the Christ Life can test every worldly-based enterprise and ego-serving endeavor of human existence. But the tests are to strengthen, not break us; nothing that opposes God's Plan of Good in any way can eventually win and, therefore, never can last.

In the mysterious Ways of God, every ending becomes a new beginning: every death a new birth, every correction a clean slate, every overcoming an elevating fresh start, every mastery an advancement into a new, higher, spiritual appointment and every passing era a transforming new age. On the Ascending Pathway Christward, there will always be another horizon to beckon us, another mountain to climb. The successful culmination of each stage of our spiritual growth also provide a rebirth into a new cycle of heightened spiritual unfoldment - qualifying us for larger spiritual assignments in further evolving our Selfhood.

The Sunlight Summit

In what has been called the "Sunlit Summit" of his spiritual understanding of the Regenerative Way of God, the Apostle Paul declared his reliance and security: "What shall we then say to these things? If God be for us, who can be against us?" (Romans 8:31). He then returned us to the central spiritual discipline (Discipleship) of this life, "And be not fashioned according to this world: but be ye transformed by the renewing of your mind, that ye may prove what is the good and acceptable and perfect will of God" (Romans 12:2).

In the ancient traditions of Spiritual Initiations, the most severe challenges and hardest tests were incorporated into the final step (The Cross) - which, when courageously and worthily met, gave release (Resurrection) and rebirth (Ascendancy) into a new, Transcendent State of Being (symbolically enacted by Three Days in a Tomb). Especially when the results of our commitment to spiritual principles, the faithful application of spiritual laws and the dedication of our lives to spiritual priorities seem long overdue, this culminating Beatitude is both an encouragement to see it through and the Divine Promise of a spiritual consummation.

In Paul's affirmations of assurance involving the Appearance: "But we all, with open face beholding as in a glass the glory of the Lord, are changed into the same image from glory to glory, even as by the Spirit of the Lord'' (II Corinthians 3:18). He rested his case with the testimonial: "Holding forth the word of life; that I may rejoice in the day of Christ, that I have not run in vain, neither labored in vain" (Philippians 2:16), "I have fought a good fight, I have finished my course, I have kept the faith" (II Timothy 4:7).

The entire Sermon on the Mount is, in fact, an ingenious Spiritual Testament of the secret creative process of Genesis: our liberation from the bondage of ignorance and introduction to an awakened consciousness of Spiritual Truth. Truth, goodness and all the qualities of higher spiritual awareness progressively invoked and unfolded through the Beatitudes make their way through the resistance of limited human consciousness in quite a predictable process. First, the persecutions come in the form of ridicule, next a fight "unto the death" - and then complete acceptance, as though it were the most obvious fact in the world.

"For this is the love of God, that we keep his commandments: and his commandments are not grievous. For whatsoever is born of God overcometh the world: and this is the victory that overcometh the world, even our faith" (I John 5:3,4).

"Who shall separate us from the love of Christ? Shall tribulation, or distress, or persecution, or famine, or peril, or sword...Nay, in all these things we are more than conquerors through him that loved us" (Romans 8:35-37).

Opposition, well met and overcome, always takes us higher on the Upward Path of God Consciousness. As we see this summit-Beatitude through to its climactic triumph, we are transposed ("Born Again") into a new point of spiritual departure - an expanded horizon (a "new heaven"), a loftier mountain to be climbed (a "new earth").

The foremost commitment in all life is to stand fast in the Spiritual Truth we presently know and allow God's Spirit within us to manifest that Truth in every situation and condition that comes into our experience - regardless! It will always take us higher. Nothing outside ourselves can long thwart or ever defeat God's Divine Plan for our highest good (again, underwritten by the universal restorative instrument of discipleship and grace for all spiritual transformation and ascendancy: ''And ye shall know the truth, and the truth shall make you free'' John 8:32).

So in all your aspirations and strivings towards the heights of Truth, always remember, ''Greater is he that is in you, than he that is in the world'' (I John 4:4). And then, ''Hangeth in there!''

Chapter Ten

The Great Prayer

Jesus' Beatitudes have provided us with a basic inner structure from which we can build a Christ Life. As a composite program for our soul growth, these Beautiful Attitudes correspondingly form the soul of His Spiritual Teachings. The remaining text of the Sermon on the Mount affords ancillary and integrative support to guide, energize, stabilize, enrich and heighten the attitudes and states of mind and heart that can lead us on the ascending path toward attaining Christ Consciousness.

Jesus considered each of us worthy and capable of reaching our destined goal as The Image and Likeness of God, "Unto the measure of the stature of the fullness of Christ" (Ephesians 4:13). So - for our highest and most all-encompassing spiritual benefit - instead of dispensing ecclesiastical dogmas, doctrines and creeds to constrain and control us, Jesus conferred an archetypal prayer: a comprehensive, Truth-filled, Spirit-affirming prayer, designed to liberate us and let us soar on our spiritual wings ("Ye shall know the truth, and the truth shall make you free" John 8:32). It is the world's best known and perhaps most prayed prayer. It is a prayer that unites people everywhere and reminds us, that before God, we are all One. It is most commonly called "The Lord's Prayer."

The word "Lord" is regarded generally as a synonym for "God." But it can have a more specific and revealing meaning: "The Law of our Being," or the Christ Principle of our Nature. This prayer is related to the Abiding, Individualized (I AM) Spirit of God that indwells us. This feature makes it an intimate and direct approach to God; a prayer that needs not subscribe to any outward religious prerequisite or intermediary. The "Lord's Prayer" transcends all differences in human belief systems and all humanly imposed limits.

Jesus' Great Prayer for us is a model prayer given in response to the Disciples' request, "Lord, teach us to pray"

(Luke 11:1). The prayer is found in both Luke's and Matthew's account of the Sermon on the Mount, but in different context and with considerable variation. It is remarkable that no other direct quotes from the Lord's Prayer are found in the rest of New Testament scripture. However, rather fascinatingly, its general construction and content greatly resemble an "Ancient Wisdom School" prayer out of the Mysteries of Egypt called "The Prayer of Light" - a prayer of identification with the One Presence and Power as a personal, living Presence within each person.

Originally, in the perennial tradition, there were probably three significant variances from the modern interpretation. Most likely the prayer was addressed in an affirmative, rather than supplicating, form. God (and the Lord'') was regarded as a Parent Spirit - both Mother and Father. Most important, it was designed to change us and not God.

This exemplary prayer is intended not to bring things to us, but to release potentials from within us. It has the potential and power to induce spiritual transformation within us by lifting our consciousness to the heights of spiritual understanding; and, in the process, incorporate God's spiritual plans, divine purposes and very nature into our human lives. It can meet each of us exactly where we are in our earth-life's experience and understanding. Yet, its highest meaning and power are found in learning to relate to God in prayer in the understanding of what Jesus meant by worshipping "in Spirit and Truth" (John 4:23).

Since the time Jesus gave humanity this prayer, millions of people have memorized the Lord's Prayer and recited it every day. This is a great tribute to the importance and prominence of this prayer in religious life. Yet, perhaps this is one of the limitations we have unknowingly rendered His exemplary prayer by weakening the meaning and restricting the effectiveness through rote repetition. As familiar as most of us are with the words, we need to bring the prayer alive by approaching it as if we had never heard it before and experience it as new and fresh every time. In order to do this, we need to have a good understanding of the meaning behind each word and phrase and of what the Spiritual Truth contained in each can convey.

The possibilities of spiritual transcendence inherent in The Lord's Prayer can connect us with the universal creative process behind the cosmos and bring the activity of God directly into our consciousness and then extend It outward through our lives. Originally, the prayer was divided into seven parts aligning It to the Genesis' Seven Steps (Days) of Creation. Later came the accustomed Protestant addendum. First, Jesus established His spiritual endorsement of this standard and method of prayer with the introduction, "After this manner therefore pray ye" (Matthew 6:9). He then began, as does all Creation, with God.

"Our Father"

The conventional masculine characterization of That One we call God as "Father" was in the tradition of an Ancient Mystery code-name to personify the mysterious, invisible, inner spiritual activity of the omnipresent Parent Spirit. It was also a reminder of the Indwelling Spirit of God working uniquely through the Logos: The I AM Center-Point Christ Identity of each person, ("The Father that dwelleth in me, he doeth the works" John 14:10). It signified the fathomless splendor of the Infinite One Presence and Power that can be personally experienced in the individual (also symbolized in the Kabbalistic AIN SOPH AUR, the American Indian "Nagual" and visually symbolized in the traditional flame often found burning in places of worship).

It also included a comprehensive representation of all the Divine Aspects of the Godhead Nature including the Divine Plural (Motherhood and Fatherhood) and the Trinity (Infinite Spirit, Divine Pattern and Creative Activity); and It affirmed all the Almighty and Universal Attributes, Qualities and Capabilities of The One as Benevolent Creator, Boundless Supply and Loving Sustainer of All - the Omnipresent SOURCE. It wipes out all primal notions of an angry, avenging, wrathful God Who rewards "favorites" and punishes the wicked with eternal "hellfire." Instead, it expresses a tender intimacy in which each person can personally relate to the Eternal God as a loving, attentive Presence; a God that, likewise, longs to be loved, not feared, in return. These two words at the beginning ensure us that each of us can raise our understanding to the loftiest conception possible of an All-Loving Deity - and know a God like that! As God's Divine Offspring, we are then reminded of the correlative Truth "Like father, like son"; each of us is "a chip off of the old block": Our Essential Nature is like God's. It also establishes the truth of our kinship with each other under the Fatherhood and Motherhood of God within the Brotherhood and Sisterhood of the human family.

In the first two words of The Lord's Prayer can be found a theology of cosmic magnitude: A Transcendent God, above, beyond, prior to, exalted above, more than and yet the essence of all manifest Creation; and, also, a God Immanent as an all-pervading intelligence, life, power and love eternally residing within the invisible side of our human nature. In other words, Jesus introduces us to a God that is always more and greater than any human concept we can comprehend or describe. Yet, He simultaneously provides a perception of God in which we can creatively relate everything in our personal lives - intrinsic and extrinsic - to the Great Divine Plan and Purpose behind all Creation.

"Who Art in Heaven"

This elaboration on God's Omnipresence tells us where to find God and what we can expect when we do. The ancient religious theory of cosmology was based on a belief that the earth was flat and the middle layer of a three-decker universe. The earth was a "vale of sorrows." Heaven was conceived of as "a place in the sky" where God (a male anthropomorphic being) and the Angels (likewise) dwelt. Based on the myth-ological, eschatological belief concerning the end of the world (borrowed from the Zoroastrian theology of Persia during the Hebrew Captivity), heaven was also the place where the righ-teous raised from the dead would live forever - rewarded with a benign, static, childishly pampered and problem-free exist-ence.

We are constantly reminded about the infamous bottom layer by the frightful speculations of firebrand preachers who hold many people under a morose spell of doom and gloom with a macabre expertise about the "lower regions" that seems to know a great deal more about "Hell" than Heaven, the "Devil" than God, and "sin and evil" than the Spiritual Potential within God's Children. Blessedly, the prevailing tendency among mainline theologians now is to accept the Bible portrayals of both Heaven and Hell as symbolic, not scientific, and regard them as states of soul rather than places.

The ignominious orthodox metaphor and "underworld" effigy for Hell, descending through the Hebrew words Gehenna and Sheol and the Greek word Hades, was obtained from an ancient sanitation operation outside Jerusalem where the city's refuse was burned in a pit; consuming the gross and leaving only the pure essence. In actuality, this sanitation operation provides a wonderfully reassuring symbol of the pervasive inner spiritual purification by which the "Fire of Spirit" transmutes the humanly corrupt into Regenerated Holiness (somewhat humbly but admirably aspired to on a sign I once saw on the back of a very dirty garbage truck: "We cater weddings!").

The original Greek meaning for "Heaven" emphasized the idea of expansion, or "expanding potential." Jesus' frequent analogies relating the infinite, indwelling spiritual potential ("The Father that dwelleth within") with the leavening power of yeast and the growth potential of seeds convey this same idea of proliferation. The arena in which we live our lives is in our consciousness. When we arrive at the soul level that can discern Heaven as the realm of God's spiritual potential within ourselves, we become aware that God is, and can only be found in our own consciousness - an open and receptive state of awareness that invites and allows God's spiritual influence to work and create in our thoughts and feelings.

We tend to overlook the vital importance of what we think and how we feel in determining the content and character of our lives, as well as the role our thoughts and feelings play in the fulfillment of our spiritually destined possibilities. It might be extremely enlightening to chart throughout the Bible all the times and ways that we are directed to take personal responsibility for the right ("righteous") use of our thinking and feeling abilities. We will then discover that we are encouraged even further to allow God's Spirit an open access into our minds and hearts for the all-important inspirational and intuitional expansion that will lift us into sequentially higher and higher states of spiritualized consciousness.

Prayer (God-directed "left-brain" linear-logical-rational thinking) and meditation (intuitive "right-brain" spiritual cognition) are, of course, activities of thought and feeling. They are the two complementary phases in the essential mental and emotional discipline by which we effectively align our thinking and feeling with Spiritual Truth. These activities also create the conscious connection with Spirit that invites a transmission of God's Light into our awareness. Paul summed it up in his letter to the Philippians when he enumerated the "tactical" qualities of righteousnesses we should cultivate in thought and feeling (the "whatsoevers": "...think on these things" Philippians 4:8) and then sanctioned the "strategic" inner goal of life, "Let this mind be in you, which was also in Christ Jesus" (Philippians 2:5). Implicit in prayer is the understanding that Heaven is found within ("Behold, the kingdom of God is within you" Luke 17:21). Accordingly, the aspiration of our prayer is to open our minds and hearts to the expanding influence of the Indwelling Qualities of Christ ("Until Christ be formed in you" Galatians 4:19). This objective introduces us to one of the most spiritually creative states of mind and heart possible. It dispels any sense of separation, increasingly brings alive our potential and establishes an intimate relationship with God that opens us to all that true prayer can do.

"Hallowed Be Thy Name"

"Goodness Is Thy Nature!" Jesus establishes once and for all the Absolute Goodness of God - no exceptions. It embraces all that can be associated with the word goodness ("Godness"): Holiness, Wholesomeness, Purity, Benevolence, Loving Kindness to the Ultimate, the Supreme, Total, All- Together, Sublimely Good Nature of God Omnipresent - in the entire Universe, and in each of us.

This focus centers our prayer in a loving, worshipful, awe-inspired respect for the Perfect Nature of all of God's attributes of life, intelligence, peace, power, substance and love waiting to come forth from within us and work all things together for the good in our own lives. From these four words, we learn to recognize and honor the Essence of Good in all things and enlist ourselves in the expression of God's Hallowedness pervading all life.

"Thy Kingdom Come

Thy Will Be Done
On Earth As It Is In Heaven''

We have made God's Will such an oppressive and heavy burden for humanity. It has become equivalent to a statement of alienation. The very mention of the words often convey an undertone of apprehension about God's disappointment and displeasure in the way we have turned out as errant, defective, prodigal offspring. A citation invoking God's Will seems to insinuate that we have tested God's patience past the limits and perpetuated some sort of celestial grudge against humanity in general - and are all but written off as legitimate heirs. The Will of God has become tantamount to God's inclination towards punishment, condemnation, retribution and (eternal!) punishment. We blame God's Will for our sicknesses, financial troubles, personal, social and national tragedies and every conceivable kind of misfortune and calamity. We even libel God's original good intention for us by branding ''natural disasters'' (our perception) as ''Acts of God.''

A Minister friend of mine recalled from his youth that, especially after the fervor of a Tent Camp Meeting, when someone would ask his mother ''How are you?,'' she would proudly reply ''I'm feeling poorly, Thank God!''

At a crescendo point in a zealous ''brimstone'' sermon forewarning the fate that awaited those bound for Hades, the listeners were dutifully apprised of the ''wailing and gnashing of teeth.'' One older man looking for an out proclaimed, ''I ain't got no teeth.'' ''Teeth will be provided!'' the preacher retorted.

There is actually very little humor to the toll this inverted distortion of God's Will has taken on the human race. The Will of God has provided license for some of the most vengeful and cruel atrocities ever inflicted in the history of humanity. Yet, reciprocally, the redemptive power of the right concept of God's Will is soul-enhancing and world-changing. Let there be no mistake about it, what we believe about the Will of God determines a great deal about how we relate to God and each other and either thwart or vivify our spiritual possibilities. God's Will (The Divine Will) is consistent with God's Nature. It represents God's perfect plan of manifest good for all creation.

God's Will is absolute good, omnipresent. Jesus never told anyone that God's Will was for them to suffer lack, hardship, sickness or failure. It is never punishment of any kind. None of these negations are within God's perfect blueprint for any part of creation. They are all secondary creations brought about through unregenerated human consciousness. Wanting things "my way," the determination of the Prodigal, is always second best in comparison to what The One Presence and Power in the Universe can provide. This is the open invitation to all our trouble, the self-willed excursion to the "Far Country" of our consciousness.

Translating the Divine Ideal of God's Will of Good ("in Heaven") into our personal human lives ("on earth") is one of the most decisive activities in true prayer ("Worshiping in Spirit and Truth" - integrating Spiritual Truth into our consciousness). Aligning our personal will to the transcendent Will of God and adapting Its Character into our consciousness often necessitates the only true sacrifice God requires of us. This sacrifice involves the surrender of our lesser ways to the Greater Good eternally established in the Divine Mind of our Creator. God always knows infinitely more than we do about what is highest and best in everything that concerns us.

The Will of God is the way the Winds of Spirit blow (John 3:8). We may not see it or anticipate it. It may not suit our own immediate plans, it may be something we have been conditioned to dread, but God's Will is forever moving toward Increasing Christhood and always leading to the perfect fulfillment of God's Great Plan and Purpose for our highest good. God's Will for each of us is to grow and progressively become in fact ("Earth") that which we eternally are in Truth ("Heaven"). Educating our minds and hearts to a working knowledge of the principles and laws of Spiritual Truth can prepare us to recognize increasingly the Divine Standard and Character of God as It is revealed and expressed in our personal experience. Perhaps one of the best confirmations that we are truly aligned to God's Will is the feeling of true peace that comes from deep within ourselves when we have chosen to accept an ideal as spiritually valid and committed ourselves to support it.

Praying "Thy Kingdom come, Thy Will be done on Earth, as it is in Heaven" is our consent to the highest use of our God-given gift of free choice, which is to allow our spiritual potential to be transposed into our earthly, everyday human lives. This segment of the Great Prayer opens our mind and heart to the exhilarating anticipation and joyous welcome of our daily expansion and evolution. God's Will perpetually provides the best possible outcome to anything that can ever happen to us - always!

"Give us this day our daily bread"

This acknowledges the ever-available abundance of the Kingdom of God that Jesus announced was "at hand." Originally, it was most likely a positive assertion: "You have already eternally provided everything that is rightful for the legitimate needs of my Soul. I can trust that what I truly need today will come forth in the most appropriate way for my highest spiritual benefit according to the capacity of my awareness." Here, Jesus is telling us that the true way to prosperity is through a consciousness that abides in the recognition of God as our Supply. In this context, "Give us this day our daily bread" can be used as a great affirmation of the spiritual principle that underlies all prosperity: "God's Heavenly Supply always equals our earthly demands." God is the universal, boundless, unfailing Source and there is nothing we shall ever need that isn't already prepared and waiting our rightful appropriation.

God's Heritage always enters the human domain first in the form of an idea. God's Way for our true prosperity is then linked with our spiritual growth and maturity (by the "right of consciousness" and the law of right use). The process usually involves converting a poverty consciousness to a prosperity consciousness. We begin by preparing to step out on faith in the Divine Law of Increase ("Give, and it shall be given unto you" Luke 6:38) through first assuming the responsibility of filling any lack in our lives by redeeming the poverty of unawareness that we have accepted in our own thoughts and feelings. Next, we establish the right inner mental, emotional and spiritual causes by which our prosperity, awaiting us in the Infinite Spiritual Reservoir of God's Kingdom of Abundance, is manifested into our lives. The possibilities are then open for achieving the most prosperous and proliferating of all states of human consciousness, the good stewardship of everything entrusted to us for our creative use and unselfish care by the All-Providing Parent Spirit.

These ideas are all contained in Jesus' lesson to the Disciples about the faithful servant and the wise steward, "And your Father knoweth that ye have need of these things. But rather seek ye the kingdom of God; and all these things shall be added to you" (Luke 12:30,31). He continues by encouraging us to further develop a grateful awareness of all the good that is currently active in our lives in the present time. He would have us look with prayerful wonder at all the blessedness that lies at hand today, fully appreciative that we are being continually supplied with exactly what we require, in just the way we really need it, for our ongoing optimum Soul growth and spiritual unfoldment - leaving us secure in this present moment and relieving us of any anxiety about the needs of the future: "Fear not, little flock, for it is your Father's good pleasure to give you the Kingdom" (Luke 12:32).

This is the way Jesus lived. He was absolutely confident of having everything He needed at the time and completely trusted that this would be everlastingly true in the future. His treasures were all "laid up" in Heaven. His riches were "toward God" (Luke 12:21). Through His teachings, Jesus emphasized that the true riches and treasures of life reside in the opulence of a consciousness that can be established and maintained in the peace, poise and trust expressed in His prayerful approach to prosperity, "Give us this day our daily bread." What wealth there is in that consciousness!

"And Forgive us our debts, as we also have forgiven our debtors"

Some prefer being "trespassers" to "debtors." Perhaps, "offenses" cuts quickest to the real issue of the pain and harm inflicted along the way by our mistakes and failings that have compromised the integrity of our True Self. The idea behind forgiveness is an exchange towards freedom: to give love for. The spiritual objective of the prayer is to allow love to take the place of all the shortcomings that have locked us into the level of our debts, trespasses and offenses. This is always a giant step forward, because it helps us find release from our everyday mistakes and also from our long-standing, often hidden, emotional bondage. In telling us to forgive "until seventy times seven" (Matthew 18:22), Jesus left no doubt about the importance of the continuous elimination of accrued negativity and undamming the creative flow. This is an exceedingly valuable prayer- tool for growth and expansion into higher levels of spiritual consciousness.

"And lead us not into temptation, but deliver us from evil"

The notion that God would ever actually lead us astray can be transcended with the translation, "Leave us not in ignorance - or any delusion or beguiling inclination in our consciousness that can cause us to deviate from the realization of our Spiritual Mission and Purpose for being in this life."

A primary temptation for the spiritual aspirant is in distinguishing between inspiration within the context of its spiritual understanding and the clever but wiley intellectual rationalizations by which it can be bent to our human designs. This is especially true regarding the temptation to take back the reigns of God's Spiritual Rulership once we have committed our lives to the Higher Path. The three **Classic Temptations** by which Jesus contrast the Christ Way with the devil's devices (our own unregenerated human stratagems), expose the some-times subtle, reassertive ways that we need to guard within ourselves in succumbing again to the notorious serpentine allurements of **wanton materialism, personality aggrandizement** and **temporal worldly power.** In Jesus' words: "No man, having put his hand to the plow, and looking back, is fit for the kingdom of God" (Luke 9:62).

For our comfort, this prayer might also be an affirmation that we will never be given more than we can handle. God has our highest good already prepared and knows all about us and what is best for us at any time. Therefore we can be certain that when an opportunity or challenge arises for us God knows that we currently possess all the capabilities we need to see it through to its good and right outcome.

Another temptation that can immobilize our spiritual endeavors is to become so involved with our "sinful ways" that our contrition diverts all our positive possibilities for virtues into a negative obsession with our faults. "The essence of evil is to think of oneself and of other people simply as perishable by-products of an impersonal nature and live accordingly. The essence of good is to think of oneself and others as Children of God, and live accordingly" (Author unknown).

Undoubtedly the most commonplace temptation is to get so caught up in the complications of our everyday living that we constrict our interests and priorities mainly to earthly "matters of consequence," more the "sin of omission than commission." "Lead us not into temptation," therefore, can be a very good cover-all prayer asking God to help us stay on the Spiritual Path.

With "but deliver us from evil," things can get really serious - theologically. The enigma and wrangles about the "primitive question" of good versus evil takes us back to Genesis and the fable of the Snake that tempted Eve. But unless we insist on languishing in the darkness, it doesn't have to be that way. Jesus set it all straight in the Sermon on the Mount when he said, "But I say unto you, That ye resist not evil" (Matthew 5:39).

To solve the ancient question of evil, we go back to "square one": "There is One Presence and One Power in the universe, God the Good, Omnipotent"! The fundamental fact of existence is that the universe is the expression of One Good God. "Evil" has no power to create itself. It is "in the eye of the beholder," meaning that it originates within unredeemed human perception ("The light of the body is the eye: if therefore thine eye be single, thy whole body shall be full of light. But if thy eye be evil, thy whole body shall be full of darkness" Matthew 6:22,23). Darkness is a biblical symbol for ignorance. That which we call "evil" results from our living in spiritual ignorance. "Evil" is Good that has been misconceived and put into expression the wrong way: "sin," which simply means "missing the mark" ("off center" of the principles and laws of spiritual truth - the spiritual knowledge that "shall make you free").

"Evil," therefore, is only conditional. It is not a thing or an entity; it is a misguided human function. Its only power is bestowed by us and, consequently, can be withdrawn by and through us. This means that, no matter how much it appears to the contrary, the power of Good (an aspect of God's Nature and Power) is always greater than any manifestation of evil. Evil can always be converted to Good. Good can always triumph!

Our greatest temptation is to fight evil. This misguided conflict often requires that we commit our religious lives to helping God out in a fight that has been conceived of as a cosmic battle between Good and Evil (Persian Dualism). Resistance just adds to the temporal strength of evil's artificial power - the only power it has - by relating to it as though it, and not Good, were the Great Reality of our existence. At the same time, it debilitates our own power to participate in the expression of true goodness. It is against the basic principle of God's Plan for manifest creation and the Law of Mind Action to believe in evil and produce good.

Paul said, "Be not overcome of evil, but overcome evil with good" (Romans 12:21). Darkness is merely the absence of light. All the darkness in the world cannot withstand the presence of the one small light. The presence of light eradicates darkness without struggle or conflict. There is nothing to oppose or combat - only a deficiency to rectify.

Similarly, evil is always overcome by active goodness - which can only occur through an inspired (enlightened) human life. Much evil has been perpetuated on the world by those who have attempted to compel "righteousness." Imposing and enforcing morality through fear and even legislation is never truly successful. True goodness can emanate only from a heart-felt desire to express and outwardly ennoble the innate Goodness inherent within everyone. "A Saint is one who makes goodness attractive" (Laurence Housman).

Nonresistance is not the toleration of evil, it is the giving of our full attention to and focusing all our energy ("Light") on supporting the Good. The "single eye" is established in the spiritual discipline of beholding only the good and upholding the divine ideal of basic goodness that lies at the heart of everything in the universe: "And God saw everything that he had made, and, behold, it was very good" (Genesis 1:31).

The Lord's Prayer is a brief, clear summation of Jesus'

teachings and a pattern for spiritual worship and devotion. "Deliver us from evil" is a summary invocation for liberation from our own ignorance and the negative states of our consciousness. Then we are free to concentrate all our interest and devote our attention to spiritual truth rather than on our mistakes, doubts, fears, wrong judgements of self and others and anything in our minds and hearts that is not in harmony with the Jesus Christ truth.

Jesus concluded His original "Lord's Prayer" by also reminding us of two major tenets of His teaching. First, all things in life, including Salvation, always emerge from within. We are "delivered from evil" - primarily an adverse state of consciousness - by holding fast to the Truth that "sets us free." Second, "The Way, the Truth, and the Life" of unfolding our Divine ("I Am") Potential is embodied only by practicing the Presence, never the absence, of God.

"For thine is the kingdom, and the power, and the glory forever"

This Protestant Doxology is an added enrichment as a final reminder of the Greatness of God and our true and wonderful relationship with God as "Children of the most high" (Psalms 82:6).

"Amen"

"It is so!": "This is now my Covenant with God," "I see it, I believe it, I live it - and that is the way it shall be forevermore!"

Chapter Eleven

The Great Paradox I
("In the World")

There came a time in Jesus' ministry when it was obvious that most of those who flocked to Him were there for the worldly "loaves and fishes." The attraction was normal enough. Most appealing might have been the corporeal healings and then the demonstrations of tangible abundance. There was also an aura of excitement.

The Miracles Jesus performed often attracted "great multitudes," many of whom expected to be entertained. There were frequent requests from the crowds to "Shew us a sign," a feat of magic commonly associated with street healers. On top of all that, for most every Jew, there would be the truly exhilarating anticipation that Jesus just might possibly be the Messiah. We see from their recorded remarks that even His Disciples were attracted mostly by the personal benefits associated with the coming of the Messiah. They increasingly voiced their frustration, even disappointment, that He seemed to delay or even avoid fulfilling these expectations. In the end, Jesus was largely misunderstood and rejected by most of the Jewish people; for, in truth, He proved to be much more of a Messiah than they actually wanted.

Jesus introduced a radical approach to life based on a new, creative relationship with God. As most of us now, the Jews of His time really only wanted someone to change the situations, circumstances and conditions in their world for them - or even more provide an evacuation out of the world. His message centered instead on the spiritual transformation of the individual and the changes that must occur within each one of us - while "in the world."

We also see from some of Jesus' admonishments to the crowds that He didn't want to be known merely as a wonder worker and "miracle man" ("Except ye see signs and wonders, ye will in no wise believe" John 4:48). In sharp contrast, He repeatedly directed us to use our potential for transformation

("**Thy** faith hath made thee whole." Matthew 9:22). All through His teaching, He dramatized the gamut of the basic problems in our lives as frustrations of our divine potential. He then taught us the spiritual process by which we can awaken to and develop our True Nature. He also perfectly Modeled the life we were all created to live from the Christ within ourselves.

Jesus linked the fulfillment of our human needs, including healing and true prosperity, with inward changes and spiritual growth. He taught that a spiritual prerequisite for meeting any need is to learn to center our faith in God, make real the eternal truths in our consciousness and to experience God's Indwelling Presence and Power as "Life more abundant" in every phase of our being.

Jesus' Transcendent Message

The high order of Jesus' teachings was recognized even by His opponents ("Rabbi, we know that thou art a teacher come from God" John 3:2). There were actually several ways in which Jesus presented His total message. A basic form of instruction was the parable, "an earthly story with a heavenly meaning," reinforced by numerous precepts of short postulates and formulas of truth. Behind the symbolic words and picturesque characters and plots that Jesus formulated into these everyday stories lies a wealth of spiritual meaning, often more than our current understanding allows. When understood in their spiritual context, they reveal a range of spiritual understanding and aid in releasing higher creative manifestations of our spiritual potential.

A second teaching method was through the practical application of Spiritual Principles and Laws in the everyday needs and problems of living. But, and apparently very disappointing to Him, most of His listeners missed the connection to their own potential and failed to grasp that the true purpose of the Miracles was to awaken them to the latent spiritual possibilities within. In fact, the success of this phase of His ministry of what appeared to be magical power begin to eclipse His Spiritual Message. At the heart of the rejection of the second Temptation was His renunciation of gaining popular appeal through enticing people to vicariously subjugate themselves to the charismatic props and allure of personality power.

As a result, Jesus initiated a third transcendent Model by which to convey "the Way, the Truth, and the Life" that He came to reveal. To bring to life the authentic Archetypal Ideal of the Christ Life that is possible for all humans, He used His Own ("Son of God") Divinity to express the qualities of Christ within the creative process of His human ("Son of man") life.

The great turning point came with His valiant decision to leave His Galilean ministry, return to Jerusalem and chart a course that would directly lead to His Crucifixion - and paradoxically, carry His ministry to its triumphant climax. With this personal example, by which Jesus bids all people to "Follow me," He became the Living Truth about the Christ Of God in every person. In the closing phases of His ministry, He shifted His emphasis almost entirely from exoteric teachings ("outer" - connectional - peripheral - extrinsic) to the esoteric ("inner" - personal - experiential - intrinsic). Everything connected with the Last Week - including the Triumphal Entry into Jerusalem, the Footwashing, the Communion, the Betrayal, Gethsemane and the Crucifixion-Resurrection-Ascension - contains symbology of the spiritual ideas, divine qualities, transformational powers and the dynamics of the inner creative process that can become active in each of us.

The Religious Overlay

Out of Jesus' life and teachings - filtered through the political and social perplexities of many centuries including the Dark Ages - evolved the religious movement and institution called Christianity, which is now separated into over 400 denominations and sects and divided by different interpretations. The world has often misunderstood Jesus and continues to misunderstand His simplest teachings. Most still look at His message through "a glass darkly" and see in it little reflected of our True Selves and what we can be. Moreover, we see in ourselves only the murky top of the waves and miss the profound depths of our Image-and-Likeness spiritual nature of the Christ within us.

Jesus counted as His Followers only those who actually practiced His spiritual way of living. There can be a vast difference between a Christian life and a Christly Life. To live a Christian life, if based on the concept of institutional once-in-a-lifetime ceremonial Salvation of what we believe to be the hopelessness of a basic faulted nature, can be to follow the Teachings of Jesus with the notion that God, Christ and Salvation are totally separate from and completely outside ourselves - "up there."

On the other hand, to live the Christ Life is to follow the teachings of Jesus with the knowledge and faith that God eternally abides in each of us as the Christ Indwelling. A Christ life focuses on a Spiritual Presence that is always ready, willing and able to express all that is needed at any time to save us from any human error. It also continually provides us with the new opportunities to learn and grow beyond whatever we transiently are in our humanity to what we can be in our Divinity - always from within. It is a major, transcending step to realize that this divine purpose and spiritual mission was not only to reveal the Divinity in Himself, but the Christ Spirit latent in all humans - to extend to all people the knowledge and promise: "Therefore if any man be in Christ (Consciousness), he is a new creature: old things are passed away; behold, all things are become new" (II Corinthians 5:17).

Paul continues: "Examine yourselves, whether ye be in the faith; prove your own selves. Know ye not your own selves, how that Jesus Christ is in you, except ye be reprobates?" (II Corinthians 13:5). Paul is telling us to "go within" and discover in our own inner nature the Image and Likeness, Seed of God's Nature, Christ Pattern that God has eternally placed within us. He is inviting us to focus our attention and faith on the inner power of Spirit to overcome our "lesser self" and bring forth the possibilities of the "Greater Self" of the Christ Spirit Indwelling.

A "reprobate" is one who rejects and refuses to sanction his or her True Spiritual Self, the only barrier that keeps the Christly True Inner Self in a dormant state. In the book of Romans, Paul further elaborates: "For they that are after the flesh do mind the things of the flesh; but they that are after the Spirit the things of Spirit" (8:5) and "For as many as are led by the Spirit of God, they are the sons of God" (8:14). There are more Scriptures in which Paul affirms the undiscerned Christ of God Image in each of us (Romans 8:9-19, 16:25; I Corinthians 2:7,14-16, 15:20-22; II Corinthians 3:8, 5:17, 6:18; Galatians

2:2O, 4:19; Ephesians 4:13,24, 5:8; Philippians 1:21, 2:15, 3:14; Colossians 1:27, 2:2, 3:1O, 4:3; I Thessalonians 5:5).

One of the unresolved paradoxes in Christianity results from the doctrinal stance which generally supports only one side of the truth disclosed in Jesus' Life: His Divinity alone. The dogma of the Church adamantly "rejects and refuses to sanction" the possibility of the dormant Christ Nature awaiting to be reborn within and expressed outwardly through each person. The result of this refutation sadly supports the inglorious untruth that repudiates our essential God-given spiritual Nature and therein unwittingly performing the very role of which it is so contemptuous, the "AntiChrist."

The Paradox - A Spiritual Sentinel

But the paradox is the relentless sentinel guarding the narrow Gateway to Higher Life entered into from a true spiritual understanding of the message of Jesus (Matthew 7:14). Half truths are not only incomplete, but deluding and often devious. In order to lead us into a holistic perception of truth ("the whole truth"), Jesus employed the paradox all through His teaching. Indeed, He loaded the Sermon on the Mount with a series of paradoxes. Few people get past the paradox without a spiritual awakening. Most theology gets trapped in the paradox. It is the most difficult barrier for religious belief systems to pass through as representatives of spiritual truth. The sentry at the gate is implicit: "Spiritual things must be spiritually discerned." Even the most intellectually learned theologians and philosophers are blocked on the frontier to true spiritual understanding.

Jesus' words often confounded His listeners. His message was simple, but only to those with the openness of spiritual discernment. And to acquire this "Pearl of great price," it is important for the serious spiritual aspirant to grasp the hard-to-explain principle involved in the paradox - seemingly self-contradictory statements, or virtues, qualities and activities that appear incompatible according to common acceptance, but that in reality contain a truth.

Jesus addressed the paradox over and over by telling us that we live in two worlds, not contradictive and forever irreconcilable, but existing simultaneously as complementary counterparts meant to work together for the Highest Good. Part of the Good News of Jesus' message is that all paradoxes can be resolved in Spiritual Truth.

Jesus not only taught in paradoxes, but His life modeled for us the Divine Paradox. Some of His references about Himself were stated as paradoxes:

"I and my Father are one" (John 10:30) - "The Son can do nothing of himself" (John 5:19); "Son of God" (once - Mark 14:61,62) - "Son of man (often); "I am one that beareth witness of myself, and the Father that sent me beareth witness of me" (John 8:18) - "Why callest thou me good? there is none good but one, that is, God" (Matthew 19:17).

Other paradoxes were incorporated into the basic teaching in His Parables. For example:

"Except a corn of wheat fall into the ground and die, it abideth alone: but if it die, it bringeth forth much fruit. He that loveth his life shall lose it; and he that hateth his life in this world shall keep it unto life eternal" (John 1 2:24).

This, one of the most commonly misunderstood paradoxes, is used to justify both the complete renunciation of the world and the relentless resistance of evil.

Another confusing paradox, in seemingly total contradiction to the Angelic Promise of the Annunciation of His Birth, "On earth peace, good will toward men" (Luke 2:14), as well as the Fifth Commandment, "Honor thy father and thy mother" (Exodus 20:12), is the startling statement:

"Think not that I am come to send peace on earth: I come not to send peace but a sword. For I am come to set a man at variance against his father, and the daughter against her mother, and the daughter in law against her mother in law" (Matthew 10: 34,35).

And the enigmatic:

"If any man desire to be first, the same shall be last of all, and servant of all" (Mark 9:35), which is inconsistent with any competitive approach to attainment. The Beatitudes were also presented paradoxically; "**Happy** are those" that are "poor in spirit," "they that mourn,"

"they which are persecuted" and so forth seems the
inversion of our values and the absolute reversal of
our goals. The paradox involving the pursuit of happiness, itself, is that it can't be achieved by taking
"dead aim" at it. True blessedness is the result of
serving something or someone else.

The paradoxes that Jesus presented in the rest of the
Sermon on the Mount are equally as confounding to rational
intelligence.
"If thy right eye offend thee, pluck it out." "If thy right
hand offend thee, cut it off." "Agree with thine adver
sary quickly", "Resist not evil...turn the other cheek,"
"love your enemies."
These are clear enough, but are never really accepted.
"Lay not up for yourself treasures upon earth...but
treasures in heaven"; "Take no thought for your
life...what ye shall eat,... drink; nor... what ye shall put
on."
If taken literally, these saying would make practical living
impossible. These concepts throwing the burden of taking care
of us on the rest of society (as well as severely oppose the
Calvinistic-Protestant "work-ethic": a ramification, coinciding with the Industrial Revolution, of the premise that "worldly
success" is a sign of being among the Predestination Select).

The face value of a companion Scripture in Matthew
19:23:
"Verily I say unto you, That a rich man shall hardly enter
into the kingdom of heaven"
has not been taken seriously by our major religions, which have
often amassed more worldly wealth than the richest commercial
companies.
"But seek ye first the kingdom of God, and his righteousness; and all these things shall be added unto you"
(Matthew 6:33)
has certainly not been given much credence in the world of
commerce.

Possibly the most ambivalent of the goals Jesus advocated for us is His summons to us:
"If any man will come after me, let him deny himself, and
take up his cross and follow me. For whosoever will save

his life shall lose it: and whosoever will lose his life for
my sake shall find it'' (Matthew 16:25,26).

Perhaps the best approach in attempting to define the
Divine Paradox is to look first at all the opposing and contrasting things in everyday life in terms of the Principle of Polarity.
In the visible realm of time and space, the familiar world of
material things, plants, animals and people, we have opposites:
dark and light, up and down, peace and war, health and sickness,
joy and pain, win and lose, active and passive, alpha and omega
and ''right brain'' and ''left brain'' - all the ''push pull'' that
provides the great drama of conflict and resolution in life.
Even as a symbol of Spiritual Destiny, the **American Eagle** is
depicted with an olive branch in one claw and arrows in the
other.   And, in actuality, it was the horrendous Civil War
that truly united the States of America into one nation.

''Spiritual Things are Spiritually Discerned''

It would be well at this point to pause and remind
ourselves that ''Spiritual things must be spiritually discerned,''
and that ''The language of Spirit is symbolism.''   In order to
follow the thread of spiritual understanding so elaborately
unfolded through the arrangement of biblical stories it is vital to
understand the methods of symbolism used to convey the
spiritual meanings of the Bible.

The Bible contains nearly every form of literature: prose,
narrative, drama, essay, short story, poetry, psalm, parable,
precept, epigram, aphorism, metaphor, fable, allegory, analogy
and apocalypse. There is also humor, figurative exaggeration,
factual and idealized history and much colloquial vernacular
and idiomatic ''slang'' - all originally woven around the Eastern, Semitic outlook. The Bible also draws vivid pictures for
spiritual correlation from familiar ordinary objects, or quickens
and colors our imagination with esoteric images and myths to
deepen perception, heighten inspiration and make abstract truth
more comprehensible. Often a name (or renaming) of a person,
a city, star, clouds, mountains, caves, rocks, thrones, seeds,
fire, weddings, food, feet, animals, mythical creatures, fantasy
realms, measurements, directions, temples, houses and even
tents are used to impart spiritual understanding, reveal concealed metaphysical knowledge and disclose mystical insights.

The Bible features metaphors, analogies and symbology. Most ubiquitous, but rarely recognized, is the codified use of single Hebrew letters and key words to enshrine truth (by the same correlation in which concurrent exoteric/esoteric knowledge was encased in Egyptian hieroglyphs). This is complemented and reinforced by epitomized numerical values that secure meaning and successively delineate understanding about important themes.

As we shall discover, some subjects, such as birth and rebirth, are restated or inferred in almost every form and image the Bible contains. Another example "water," beginning in Genesis with the "face of the deep," is repeated many times in terms of seas, lakes, rivers, wells, waterpots, cups, baptism, "water made wine" ("Communion"), "living water" and so forth, always representing some state, activity or quality of consciousness.

The relationship of numbers (a universal language), starting in the Seven Days of Creation, is dispersed throughout the entire Bible. This ancient and masterly symbolism is distinctively precise and consistent in sustaining the meaning of important truths unaltered by misunderstandings in translation or differences of opinion. Yet, we have often missed seeing the forest for the trees.

An initial point of reference is the symbolic representation of the numbers **One** and **Three**. This contrast is found in the doctrinal divergence between the Hebrew concept of **One God** and the Christian **God in Three Persons**. The Principle of Divine Oneness, contained in the Monotheism of Moses, and the trinitarian formula for the Universal Creative Process within the One Great Unity pervading the Whole, adapted from the Great Mysteries and fully accepted as Church Dogma in the 4th Century, are really only different perspectives of the Living God. Both concepts are quite compatible in transcendent Spiritual Truth. The Sacred Knowledge for perceiving the Three-In-One activity of Spirit manifesting the Divine Image of the One Supreme Being, a divine expression of Perfect Potential-Perfect Pattern- Perfect Power, is most familiar as Father-Son-Holy Spirit (originally Father-Mother-Holy Child). This triune relation can also be applied metaphysically (Mind-Idea-Expression) and individual to our threefold nature (Spirit-Soul-Body).

The Cryptic Keys to Creation

To start from the beginning, in the First Genesis Story of Creation, we are introduced (the First Day) to the great **Universal Truth Principle of Oneness ("1")**: "In the beginning God...". (In a Declaration of Unity, Paul offers a splendid compendium of the Universal Oneness of Creation: "One Lord, one faith, one baptism, One God and Father of all, who is above all, and through all, and in you all" Ephesians 4:5-7).

This idea was followed on the Second Day (when the Waters of Divine Consciousness were divided) by the disclosure of the **Polarity Principle ("2")**; the two-fold origin of manifestation and proliferation. This creative union of dual counterparts was later restated "Male and female created he them" (not "two plus two," but the multiplying power of two complements unified) and reiterated with special emphasis on the great story of consciousness cleansing and renewal when Noah loaded the Ark "Two and Two."

"Two" misconceived is **"uncreative" duality** - eating the blemished fruit of our negative perceptions of "naming" things adversely. This is the untrue and illusionary basis from our unfledged free-willed choice for overshadowing life with the calamitous belief in separation from God; and the false premise and artificial genesis of the Reality of **"evil"** (**"live"** conceived backwards) in the Divine Creative Process.

Historically, from "2" on, almost every phase of humanity's existence has tended to be disproportionately oriented outward to the visible world of material properties and physical appearances that exist within the dualistic table of limitations of our third dimensional ("3"), five-senses based understanding ("5") gained exclusively from exterior facts and the externally conditioned opinions "of the world."

Sequentially, the Bible symbology of the number "3," when rightly conceived and generatively propagated from "2" in a "marriage" relationship of complementary opposites, then represents an "after their kind" seed-potential for creative synthesis. The mystical **"3"** ("Trinity") represents the **Universal Process of Creative Evolution.**

The number "4" (Fourth Day) symbolizes the invisible "**Four Square**" **foundation** of luminous spiritual elements from which all manifest creation is built and rebuilt.   These components include the "Greater light" (Sun) radiance of Light, Life, Truth and Love, formed and developed in "phases" (echelons and cycles of organization) as the "Lesser Light" (Moon); reflecting the Most High (Stars) in the physical elements of "fire, air, earth and water" within the symbolic metaphysical construct ("Firmament of the heaven") of "East, West, North and South."

The number "5," such as the Five Books of the Law of Moses, David's Five Smooth Stones of Truth in his "duel" with Goliath, or the Five Loaves in feeding the Five-thousand, pertain to our involvement in the tangible world of objects, people, governments, institutions, property, fame and fortune. We tend to consider the objects to be "reality" and are apt to use them as a gauge for all our values and accomplishments and accept them as the goals and purposes of our existence.

"5" (our **terrestrial trainingfield for soul development**) represents human life experienced on and usually limited to the level of our five sense's form-existence.   Human life, therefore, is usually engrossed in acquiring material goods. Especially in the rise of scientific exploration, humanity had come to believe almost exclusively in the supreme dominion of the "facts" of our five senses. Religion, on the other hand, still tends to regard any higher creative expression or spiritual transcendence in a pre-Copernican mode of "supernatural."

With sword-like incisiveness, Jesus contrasted this finite perception with the assertion that the true reality of life is discovered only in the awareness that there is also a Spiritual Kingdom "At hand" and "Within you." Jesus then redirected us to the First Day Principle of Oneness ("1") and the Divine Basis of all things in God.   Accordingly He taught that all life emanates from the invisible side of Creation, an unformed, non-material, Spiritual World behind, beneath and interpenetrating the visible world. He revealed this Spiritual Domain as the One Universal Source-Essence ("Father") that supports and gives substance to all that is manifested - guided by One Transcending, Omniscient Intelligence that originates, evolves and completes all that is. (As the Little Prince learned: "That which is essential is invisible to the eye''.)

Many of the secrets of the universe have remained hidden from us because we have misconceived all things by their appearance ("2") and lived only in a fixed world perceived of as solid matter. But, with Einstein's E=MC² breakthrough trinity formula of Relativity ("3"), we have learned that all manifest forms and relationships are from one radiant energy vibrating at varying rates of speed. Today scientists are learning more and more and almost daily expanding our concept of God's invisible creation and powers in the universe.

Jesus especially emphasized that the Originating Source of the Godhead ("1") and the Divine Cybernetics and Corrective behind all manifestations ("4") is not detached in a far-off, distant sky, but right here all the time. This Divine Fount is the larger, deeper, abiding Dimension of Spirit to which we can be mystically "born" and become a "new man." "The Kingdom of God" (Jesus' distinction for this Spiritual Realm of existence) is the One, eternal, infinite, omnipresent, uniformly unmanifested Divine Essence. Again, by contrast, all things on the physical plane ("5") exist within a collaborative process of pairs ("2"); polar opposites in quality and activity, yet incomplete and absolutely dependent upon the other (relative) as an interrelated counterpart for creativity combining ("3") and becoming whole.

In summary, the first five steps in the Creative Process of Genesis reveal:

("1") (Monad) the Foundation of all Creation is the One Omniscient, Omnipotent, Omnipresent Spirit of God - the Supreme Good;

("2") (Dyad) the Activity of God works through the Law of Polarity, in which opposites attract that they might unite and become more than the sum of the original parts (such as with an electric battery; or better yet, in biblical symbology, a "Marriage made in Heaven");

("3") (Triad) the Higher Union is fulfilled through through the Creative Trinity Formula: the synergy of counterpole components integrating to form a higher state of truth and wholeness, "thesis-antithesis-synthesis."

("4") (Tetrad) the built-in provision for all correction, atonement, and upward renovation is through Regeneration (Rebirthing) - a return to Spiritual "Square One" and a perennial new start within the timeless context of the first **four words** of the Bible, "In the beginning God";

("5") (Pentrad) the manifest side of creation (and our "In the world" earth-life as symbolically represented in the Second Creation Story of Genesis) as a continual interplay between the polarity of contrasting forces enduringly at work in helping evolve God's Spiritual Plan for an upward, onward, perfecting tangible expression of Wholeness (Oneness) in the Universe.

The Fall and Rise of Man

Now, with these paradigmatic and symbolic keys, to get to the roots of the human predicament of our longstanding bondage to a belief in separation (arresting the Creative Process at "Second Day" negating-duality), we need to resolve the paradox of the "Apple Tree Story." This mythological tradition is common to several cultures; and, through misinterpretation, has been primarily responsible for most religious misinterpretation and misunderstanding. This ancient story was presented in allegorical form to give insight to the process of spiritual growth, from an infant to a mature consciousness, set in motion when we first entered into the world of opposites by evolving from "paradisaic" instinctive living into "reflective consciousness."

The **thesis** centers around the God-given gift of Selfhood (manifested as "ego" = "me," or to know one's uniqueness). This divine endowment inaugurated the inestimable co-creative possibilities of self-expression vested in our Individuality; and its bequest of unbounded ability to choose ("name things") coupled with the awesome responsibility for the "fruits" of our choices. It poignantly dramatizes our **antithetic** inner disorientation and trauma when we are first faced with the necessity to overcome both our initial limited states of unknowing (''innocence'') and the infantine stages of our seductive, self-centered, lower ego nature seeking to extend itself (''Snake'').

Intertwined in the classic ''Tree Of Life'' theme is our Spiritual Summons to assume responsibility for gaining valid knowledge for our **synthesist** growth and spiritual fruition through experiencing and mastering the lessons unique to earthlife. Therein, we are able to transmute our beginning negative human perception of duality that result from spiritual ignorance into a blossoming creative consciousness of Spiritual Oneness. This new consciousness will, in turn, nurture a corresponding growing expression of our True Nature and Basic Goodness (''Blessed is the man that walketh not in the counsel of the ungodly...And he shall be like a tree planted by the rivers of water, that bringeth forth his fruit in his season; his leaf also shall not wither; and whatsoever he doeth shall prosper'' Psalms 1:1,3).

It is important to note that the ''Tree of Life'' (''The Life of Spirit'') and the ''Tree of Knowledge of Good and Evil'' (life by trial and error) grow together in the midst of the Garden, central to our life's experience. Our (Augustine's) idea of the ''Fall'' as the denigration of the human race is a major delusion brought forward by an incapability to grasp the Principle of the Paradox. The Garden of Eden story relates Its message unmistakably to humanity's evolving understanding of Spiritual Truth with Its ending:

''And the Lord God said, Behold, the man is become one of us, to know good and evil: and now, lest he put forth his hand, and take also of the tree of life, and eat, and live for ever: Therefore the Lord God sent him forth from the garden of Eden, to till the ground from whence he was taken. So he drove out the man; and he placed at the east of the garden of Eden Cherubims, and a flaming sword which turned every way, to keep the way of the tree of life'' (Genesis 3:22-24).

A tree, from the Third Day of Creation, is a wonderful analogy for revealing the secrets of the spiritually energized growth process in life with all its intricacies, complexities and contingencies from seed to fruition. The acquisition of true knowledge (Enlightenment) is correspondingly a growth and development process.

Most people like to "know," but often resist and resent the process of having to learn. Yet, developing valid spiritual understanding involves far more than cursory head-knowledge. It entails the disciplined application of tenets of Spiritual Truth to the crucible of our daily living and the demonstration of their virtue and integrity in the practical experiences of our human lives - until they are **comprehended** in their spiritual context (devoutly beheld and revered: "The beginning of wisdom" Psalms 111:10), **realized** (Born Anew in us as spiritual reality) and fully **assimilated** into the activity of our consciousness as consecrated treasures of spiritual perception brought forth in our lives ("Ye shall know them by their fruits" Matthew 7:16). Learning and developing can be two of our greatest joys. It is for this that God bestowed us with our humanity and provided its empirical, down-to-earth framework of time, space and material manifestation. But, there are no bonafide shortcuts to divine knowledge and spiritual growth.

The story of Eden, therefore, is also an amazing depiction of how we are protected from premature expression of our latent Godlike potential in ways detrimental to ourselves and others until we reach a mature consciousness of spiritual perception. Unforgettably characterized is the temptation by the serpentine beguilement of our lower sense-bound consciousness to experience life solely through the self-centered interests of our worldly desires before we attain the understanding of Truth and the paradox involved in both the privilege and responsibility of our divine heritage: "Now I say, That the heir, as long as he is a child, differeth nothing from a servant, though he be lord of all: But is under tutors and governors until the time appointed of the father. Even so we, when we were children, were in bondage under the elements of the world" (Galatians 4:1-3).

The polarity principle is allegorically incorporated into the story as a masculine and feminine pair of opposites in its most natural human representation, Adam and Eve. The principle is also translatable into an understanding of the important creative relationship (again, relativity) between our intellectual (male-objective) and emotional (female-subjective) natures. The story also ingeniously exhibits the psychological victim-defense-stages involved in the dilemma of the levels of consciousness that feel separated and alienated (''fallen''); first as guilt (''nakedness'') and then blame (''the serpent'').

Being sent forth from the Garden of Life (the Spiritual Potential for God's Creative Activity within us) to ''till the ground'' is the means God provided us to utilize the opportunity of the earth-life world of opposites to cultivate and develop our consciousness in ways that can be achieved only through the fruits of human experience. Although we have tended to undervalue and depreciate our world-based life, this is what our humanity is all about - a rare and precious gift with which to learn and grow and eventually enter into a Co-creative Partnership with God. The Creation Story establishes our humanity as a very important creative phase of our Being.

The Cherubims at the East of Eden are emblematic of God's Divine Guardianship of our spiritual evolution through the human experience and the assurance of an Entranceway from the Inner Path into the Promised Land of Spiritual Consciousness. In Biblical symbology, ''East'' (the direction of the rising sun - awakening Spiritual Consciousness) means the Source ''Within.'' Cherubims are a High Order of Angelic Beings closely connected with the ''Holy of Holies,'' the Innermost Abiding Place of God's Spirit in each individual - the I AM Immediate Presence of God Within - Who function as Emissaries and Bearers to the approach of the Throne (Presence) of God. They are also associated with constant prayers of praise (''Worshipping in Spirit and Truth''), one of the supreme enhancements to spiritual growth. Cherubims are symbolized as winged creatures and placed in pairs on each side of the Ark as figures ten cubits high, the symbolic mark of exalted Spiritual Stature.

The ''Flaming Sword'' is the Guardian vested in the Sacred Power of spiritualized free-will choice that uncompromisingly divides and protects Spiritual Truth from all untruth. The Genesis account of Creation is a medium used to set forth fundamental Spiritual Truths about the human participation in the Creative Process. It is not intended to present a factual or scientific account of our origins, it is designed to lift us into a higher level of Truth (''For the letter killeth, but the spirit giveth life'' II Corinthins 3:6). Biblical literalism has produced a great deal of our religious negative misconception and bewilderment about God's True Nature as well as ours and misled us into shamefully neglecting the sacred obligation of the dominion entrusted to us in our planetary home (reference Genesis 1:28).

The Creative Word - Noun and Verb

As a pattern for the Polarity Principle, the narrative of the Genesis Creation Story is separated into two main divisions. The first half, Genesis One, can be regarded as the Noun of Creation. It presents insights into the behind-the-scenes original plan and spiritual blueprint in terms of perfect ideas held in God's Infinite Mind for the purposes, procedures and destined fulfillment of all that God intends for Creation. It exists eternally perfect in the boundless, unfathomable, omnipresent Realm of Spiritual Potential which Jesus sometimes referred to as "The Kingdom of God." It is God's "Let there be" of Creation.

In contrast, Genesis Two represents the active, kinetic side of Creation. It depicts the way God births, evolves and fulfills Creation from Its Noun State to the Verb Form of the Creative Process. It is the Divine "To be" of Creation.

The Mission of Jesus was to connect us to the **"Noun"** principle of our being as the Image and Likeness of God (the Central **"I"** of God's Spirit Indwelling) and inspire us to take up His Identification ("Cross") as the **"Verb"** (Divine Logos **"AM"** by bringing forth God's Will (Perfect Plan of good, omnipresent) into manifestation: "Thy kingdom come. Thy will be done in earth, as it is in heaven" (Matthew 6:10). Truth is usually learned as a Noun, but can best be understood and related to as a Living Spiritual Verb Process by which God is expressed through us ("The Word made flesh").

Conversely, our inversion of "evil," which has no self-originating foundation in Creation, into a secondary-creation "noun," empowers it as a quasi-deified entity (Satan). We have delegated this personification of iniquity with idolatrous human importance in our lives ("believing in the Devil" as a power to fight) rather than recognizing it as a misshapen "verb" form of false belief (non-truth) activities. This illusory importance has diverted and thwarted our own divine imperative of being about our "Father's business" (Luke 2:49) as creative centers of spiritual activity in our own lives and world. Resisting and combating evil only darkens our vision and blinds us to THE Great Reality of our lives that Jesus came to reveal to each of us ("The mystery which hath been hid from ages..." Colossians 1:26,27): We are the divinely intended Creative Apex for manifesting God's Plan for the supreme good.

The Mystery Made Manifest

We now arrive at the crux ("Cross") of the Divine Paradox. **It is us!** As spiritual beings that have entered into the human realm of experience, we embody the paradox: we are both divine and human - and, we must learn to function as both. This is what Jesus Modeled so perfectly as both the "Son of God" and the "Son of man." Our special dignity has also been the point of our greatest failure. Our religious dogmas, doctrines and creeds have rarely connected our human lives to the Spiritual Reality of our True Nature. The world of human existence has been irreconcilably contrasted to the "Heavens" of Spirit with no understanding that they are interpenetrating and complementary. Augustine's doctrine of total human depravity and bondage to the flesh has undermined all our human endeavors to look at ourselves in terms of our Spiritual Potential and to begin to live accordingly.

This is the odd paradox in life: we involve ourselves with "tilling the ground" with all sorts of diversionary endeavors without recognizing or achieving anything for which we have been given the opportunity to embody in the physical plane of existance and develop all the advantages that our humanity affords. This earthlife provides a spiritual training ground for soul growth. The opportunities for cultivating this are as wide as the world, often unexpected and wonderful.

The chief obstacle for soul growth is wrought by us. God created us with Christlike potential. When we chose to dispute and tamper with the dignity of that Image, we are interfering with the entire creative work of God and we invite spiritual failure and personal degeneration. This trespass takes away the all-important faith in the Truth about God and ourselves. We are trapped in the limited and negative views of the world of our senses. But this human tragedy is not at all the final "Judge ment'' about the redeeming (''reclaiming our original birth-right'') possibilities in our human lives. And yet, rather par-adoxically, the resolution is actually to be found in the original Sanskrit word for judgement: ''To esteem oneself as won-drously made'' - ''And ye shall know the truth, and the truth shall make you free'' (John 8:32).

First, we must recognize that the basis for our human dilemma (''Fall'') is really our rejection of our Spiritual Poten-tiality: descending from the truth about ourselves as God's Image into a degrading mortal sense of identity. The true fulfillment of all our God-given aspirations depends upon awak-ening to, stirring up and then expressing our latent Divine Nature. We are well endowed by our Creator and much is not only possible, but expected. We must, above all, learn to see our lives in the light of our divine purpose.

It is in the reconciliation of the two aspects of our being - our human and divine natures - that the Mystery, the Secret of Life, the Divine Paradox is revealed. Paul defines our dual nature as the ''natural man'' and the ''spiritual man,'' some-times referred to as the ''outward man'' and the ''inward man,'' and then he sets forth the transformation process for reconcili-ation and atonement:

> ''And so it is written, The first man Adam was made a living soul; the last Adam was made a quickening spirit. Howbeit that was not first which is spiritual, but that which is natural; and afterward that which is spiritual...And as we have born the image of the earthly we shall also bear the image of the heavenly'' (I Corinthians 15:45-49).

This creative duality is involved in the polarity process of spiritual transformation: the possibilities between what **now is** on our present level of expression and the potential of what **can be** ''From on high.'' Especially the writings of John and Paul symbolically present this affirmative duality. These symbols include the metaphysical dynamism between the attain-ment of a Godly life based on the ''light'' (illumined conscious-ness) and a life that is bound to the ''darkness'' of human unawareness (ignorance), world- clouded misperceptions (Illu-sions) and selfishness (Satan - ''The prince of Darkness''). With this understanding of the overcoming principle inherent in

this synthesizing dualism comes the realization that there is
nothing to resist or fight, only something to know and express.

Personality and Individuality

Let's look at our lives in terms of these two aspects of
our nature, referred to in some traditions as "Personality" and
"Individuality," and investigate this contradictory being of
ours for an overview of the ways in which we sell ourselves
short; and, most importantly, to find out what the Real You is
like - and could be in your life.

Our Individuality is the easier of the two to define and the
more difficult to really comprehend. It is our original God-
begotten Image and Likeness; our Divine Sonship Nature, the
Christ of God "Within" that is our Eternal "Hope of glory."
When it is awakened to and given spiritual birth in our human
lives, It becomes some component and degree of God's "Only
Nature" in expression. It is the Divine Image we see in Jesus!

Our Personality on the other hand, from the Greek
"persona" for mask, is what hides our True Nature from view.
It acts as a changing facade of personal characteristics. Throughout life, we acquire and develop many personalities (selves).
We accomplish this by attaching our human ego to various
identities that we alternately would like to project about ourselves in meeting diverse situations and circumstances that arise
in our lives, very often in conformance to "what others might
think." This desire to conform accentuates the human part of
us, the exterior, changeable mixture of "wheat and tares,"
ordinarily (seemingly) governed by our intellect and empowered by our emotions, often in contradiction with each other.
Our personality also tends to be a "front man," masquerading
feelings of fear, separation and inadequacy. It generally
postures itself in the "victim" role and often compensates by
tangentially reflecting defensive and aggressive traits. It is
usually engrossed in material acquisition, with most of its
values based on externals. Personality goals are nearly always
centered on self-gratification. The "worldly" personality,
unaware of its True Nature and spiritual purpose in life, invents
hundreds of false and artificial existences.

Most personalities are characterized by duality. Even in

the worldly successful life, there is a baffling blend of "good" and "bad," brilliance and stupidity, greatness and smallness, magnificence and pettiness, courage and cowardice, assurance and doubt, joy and sorrow, hope and despair, faith and anxiety, loyalty and falseheartedness, trust and jealousy, charm and crudeness, generosity and greed, kindness and cruelty, friendliness and hostility, winsomeness and repulsiveness, saintliness and degeneracy and love and hate (fear) - all in the same person. In other words, our personality, as an aggregate of our human characteristics, is a conglomeration of paradoxes and, often, dissipated talents. But, our personalities are basically vehicles for our soul-development and, as such, are perfectible.

"Know Thyself"

We can now appreciate the importance of the Greek idea "Know thyself." The dominion we were gifted through our "Sixth Day" Creation in God's Image is always first established within ourselves as the mastery over our own thoughts and feelings. This inner command, in turn, builds the consciousness and then the externalized world in which we live. Entering our inner world introduces us to another strata of polarity: the intellectual (conscious) and emotional (unconscious) phases of our mind. This inner exploration also opens us to the vast realm of the invisible, sometimes referred to as "metaphysical" ("beyond the physical"), most appropriately regarded as the study of the principles and laws of that which is "not seen" - the intrinsic "Within." To establish an understanding of the paradox involved in this often mysterious domain of Creation that extends from one of the most common and constant, yet frequently overlooked, activities in everyday human living (thinking and feeling) into the infinite reaches of Universal Mind and the Absolute ("that which cannot be named"), we can divide the unseen into two complementary counterparts: **"The Science of our Thoughts and Feelings"** and **"The Mystical."**

The Science of Thought and Feeling - which of course belongs to the human side of the paradox and is our personal sphere of operation and responsibility - is the study and application of an orderly body of knowledge in both the composition and renovation of a mind and heart as proper instruments for expressing ourselves as Creative Co-partners with God. The key to this mental and emotional dominion and authority is found in the use of free choice to control the thoughts with which we weave the tapestry of our lives. The basic tenet of this metaphysical Science is the amazingly unrealized dictum: "Life Is Consciousness." Thought controls our world and each of us has been given the power to control our thoughts.

Our thinking process is not a secondary function to the more apparent and objectified undertakings in our lives. Nor is "improving our minds" simply a pastime. Taking command of our inner life and being in charge of its operation is the foremost priority, not only for spiritual ascendancy, but for any level of true mastery in living. We perpetuate severe repercussions on ourselves and the world by both neglecting and giving over to others the power to righteously control our thoughts.

It is not easy to control the activity of our mind and heart. Our inner world of thought and feeling is very complex. Our intellectual and emotional natures often have diametrically opposing tendencies ("uncreative" duality). The human intellect (the masculine principle directed by logic and rational, linear, deductive, left-brained, objective thinking) tends to take its identity and all of its interests and values from a "natural man" ego attachment. The unconscious sector of this inner kingdom (our emotional and intuitive feminine, right-brain, subjective feelings) holds a whole world of secret desires, drives and frustrations that constantly colors and subtly governs our behavior. The human mind makes a wonderful servant, but a terrible master. Louisa May Alcott once wrote: "A little kingdom I possess, where thought and feeling dwell, and very hard the task I find to governing it well." We can't claim the rights of consciousness without earning them. It takes education, discipline and growth to earn the right. "Tilling the ground" of our consciousness is a full time job. The legitimate business on the human side of Co-creation is the cultivation and integration of our own "Little Kingdom."

We alone are responsible for the training of our intellect: the discipline of learning, reasoning, deducing, appraising and separating the mental "wheat from the tares." It is the intellect that must take the initiative in courting and wooing emotions that will give positive support to our mental concepts and bring about an inner "marriage" of harmonious, creative union between the male (active) and female (responsive) counterparts of our mental-emotional "household." It must also inaugurate the process of redeeming the emotional wounds and inhibitions from our past. Then comes the important follow-through of relearning and activating new qualities of thought and feeling that foster a progressive realization of Spiritual Truth and a maximally practical and creative life - all in optimum cooperation with God in the unfoldment and molding of our Destinies.

Life's Two Basic Choices

To make the process a little less complicated, we can narrow the control of our lives and our entire human dominion and mastery down to two ever-accessible mental tools (the basis of all computer programing) contained within God's Gift to each of us of Free-Willed Choice ("Naming" things - a capacity that could never be designed into any computer): the two short and simple words **"yes"** and **"no."** In God's divine design for us, by the discipline (Discipleship) of saying "yes" to the good, the true, the beautiful, the Godlike and Christly qualities of life and "no" to all that is less, we have the capacity at all times to prepare our minds and hearts and open our whole consciousness to the inspiration and spiritually creative power of God's Infinite Intelligence.

A system of denial and affirmation for cleansing and reprograming our consciousness for spiritual transcendence is implied in all religious disciplines. The Kabbalah ("To Receive," as Inner Truth vs outer form), the mysticism of Judaism - long kept secret - has a well-guided rigorous program for resolving inner conflicts in preparation for transformation. Sigmund Freud, founder of psychoanalysis, covertly introduced this discipline into the modern science of our minds. The Twelve Step Programs for addiction recovery, for example, employ spiritual techniques evolved from the ancient Mystery School Initiations for surrendering, evaluating, correcting, cleansing, releasing and recommitting one's life to a "Higher Power." John the Baptist inaugurated the more confrontational fear-incentive for change: "Repent" (literally "rethink") "or else!". There is also the catharsis accomplished through Confession. Currently, there are other viable techniques for "getting rid of the garbage" and reentering life from a new perspective, with spin-offs on "weight loss," "success motivation," "prosperity," etc.; and some that exploit and violate our spiritual autonomy, inner sovereignty and personal responsibility by diverting control to persons or institutions outside ourselves. A good "rule of thumb" is simply never let anyone or anything come between you and your God, especially the all-important spiritual contact with God within yourself.

In reviewing the Beatitudes of Jesus, we see that He comprehensively and creatively incorporated within them all these resolving, relinquishing, purifying, unifying, liberating and transforming methods for removing the inner barriers from our True Self and leading us into a new mind and heart with a New Spirit. Any system of spiritual discipline should be carefully measured (as with religious Canon) against the divine standard of motives, methods and qualities of the Sermon on the Mount; especially for the considerations involving the Divine Paradox that are not usually obvious to the "natural man's" understanding.

Life's True Purpose

When you think about it, life "in the world" is such a curious mix of general experience for all of us, with unique and often peculiar conditions and particulars for each of us. We are created equal, but we do not stay that way very long. There is a strange inequality to the way the advantages and challenges are dealt out. Close observation of even those fortuitous few who seem to have everything (a very appealing attraction to the human ego), shows imbalances of experience, gaps of understanding and unresolved fears, faults, failings and frustrations that indicate that much is missing. "In the world" we cannot "have it all" - nor should we want to - for that is not what this earth-life is about at all. Surely in God's Infinite Intelligence, if the intended purpose were to simply lavish "everything" into our lives, a much easier and more effective system could have been preordained than going through all the restrictive conditions and challenges we are required to meet and master!

What are lavished on us in this life are the opportunities we need to fulfill its true purpose. It is actually the gift of our "in the world" limitations, including those of our physical size, senses, brain capacity, environment, earthly conditions, situations, circumstances and time and space dimensions, that are the very assets that establish our perfect personal curriculum in this life. These temporal demarcations provide the precise conditions and circumstances by which our talents and highest possibilities can be specialized into maximum opportunities for learning and growing. Just as Creation Itself is complete and perfect in Spirit - yet unfinished in the evolving process of Its manifestation - we also are, indeed, unlimited in spiritual potential. But nothing is more useless and merely speculative to us than our Potential until it is activated, practically applied and specifically developed in our lives.

The law of life is growth. Much of our life is an education for growth. We often have years of academic, cultural, social and sometimes religious training to prepare and develop us for our role in life. It is said that the good life involves continuous learning every day of our lives.

The "personality," however, tends to focus exclusively on human-ego concerns: self-security, self-interest and self-promotion - usually linking everything to careers and life-styles and learning to market ourselves like soap, or even used cars. At times, the Science of Thought and Feeling is used in an attempt to license these "in the world" exploits as "Divine Enterprises" by wrapping them in a cloak of spirituality. We never fool the Universe. Nor do we ever successfully mentally manipulate our way past the Sentinel of the Great Paradox. "Be not deceived; God is not mocked: for whatsoever a man soweth, that shall he also reap. For he that soweth to his flesh shall of the flesh reap corruption; but he that soweth to the Spirit shall reap life everlasting" (Galatians 6:7,8). The remedial curriculum will be repeated over and over, if necessary, until we achieve the true and abiding aspirations and enduring spiritual objectives necessary for our destined soul progression.

In this identity as the "natural man," the dilemma of the Great Paradox is that we concentrate all our concerns and the powers of our inner creative facilities (including imagination, faith, zeal, understanding, love and, especially will power) to pursue and strive for temporal security and fleeting benefits that "moth and dust doth corrupt" (Matthew 6:19), often with the ultimate reward of a "testimonial dinner" and a nice eulogy. Occasionally, we stop and ask, "What is life all about, anyway?" Jesus brought the true and full answer. He never in any way presented earth-life as a perfect place to have just what we want, when we want it, the way we want it. He did, often, present it as a perfect place to fully utilize the lessons unique to our lives for Soul-growth and Spiritual Development - ''Apple Trees'' and all. He demonstrated over and over that the special experiences in our individual lives are their own rewards.

Jesus' message is compelling and uncompromising: The ''not of this world'' Spiritual Imperative and the ''in the world'' Manifest Destiny of our being requires us to continuously make it the cardinal concern and the Divine Enterprise of our lives to convert all the treasures of our earthly experience into ''treasures in heaven.''

Chapter Twelve

The Great Paradox II
("Not Of This World")

Let us now integrate and fully sanctify our exploration of the Great Paradox through the recorded experience of a successive line of outstanding Bible Personages. We will introduce the theme with Nicodemus, the cautious Pharisee on the verge of spiritual perception, with whom Jesus shared one of His greatest manifestos for living "the Way, and the Truth, and the life": "Except a man be born again, he cannot see the kingdom of God" (John 3:3). The magnificence and splendor of being "Born again" needs to be lifted out of its parochial, often exceedingly self-righteous connotation and seen in its transcendental significance in relation to the spiritual birthing of the Divine in every human. The Second Birth is the awakening to the Spiritual Self and the regeneration of the "Natural man" personal-ego into the "Spiritual man" Christed-Ego.

The Great Paradox about the mystical transformation from Personality to Individuality converges around Jesus' eloquent symbol, "born anew": an emblem of spiritual transformation. The one thing humans cannot do regarding their own soul-development is cross the Frontier into Spiritual Consciousness and achieve Spiritual Transformation under the direction of the intellect alone. The resolution of the Paradox transpires through a quantum leap in consciousness. The Science of Thought and Feeling can take a personality to the Border, but it cannot gain entrance into the Mystical Realm of Spirit without being "endued with power from on high" (Luke 24:49). The Mystical, by definition, is this: "Having a spiritual meaning or reality that is neither apparent to the senses or obvious to the intellect." It is a transforming experience of Higher Consciousness, outside the fields of five-sense perception and ordinary reasoning, resulting from direct Communion with God - which inwardly and intimately relates the individual to Ultimate Reality.

The Bible Adventure

The Bible actually concentrates on a few Gemstones of Spiritual Truth, presented in many different forms and in a variety of stories in order to reach as many levels of understanding as possible. The spiritual objective and creative purpose of every symbolic representation and analogical model in the Bible is to help each individual both translate the unique situations, circumstances and personal experiences of his or her life into crucial lessons of soul growth and quicken and nurture transformational spiritual awareness.

One of the signs of true creative thinking and an awakening spiritual consciousness is in recognizing the rungs of intricate connections and maturative lineage between Bible stories and Scriptural symbology that previously seemed unrelated. We will follow an abridged path of the elaborate biblical evolvement of the mystically transcendent "Second Birth" from the Genesis Creation Account (our Original Birth in God's Image and Likeness) to the emblematic descent of the New Jerusalem in the Book of Revelation.

In this great Biblical adventure of spiritual education, preparation and transformation, it will be important to remember that the Way of the Christ is really an inner path in consciousness. It is also important for good Bible study to understand the invaluable guidance of symbology, perceive growth and development, recognize the inner causes behind outer effects, the consequences of ignorance, the ramifications of choices and divergent beliefs, and further, observe reactions as well as actions.

We return to Genesis and find that right after leaving the Garden of Eden, now "on our own" (in the infancy of our belief in separation) things quickly go from bad to worse: alienation, dissension, and defiance. It all hits bottom with the shameful incident of Cain and Abel.

Then begins the long journey of regeneration with all its "ups and downs" and pendulum swings. First, there is the inaugural "baptismal" cleansing of the cradle delusions of civilization with the great Flood and the renewed promise contained in Noah's Ark (the refuge of "two and two" for rebirthing a new state of consciousness). This is followed by a stage of further confused understanding and separation represented in a failed effort to impetuously and prematurely attain the primeval human misconceptions of an externalized Heaven by building the Tower of Babel.

The Patriarchs

Then, with Abraham's "Call" and Covenant based on the birth of awareness of the One God, dawned the major Foundation Truth Principle of Oneness ("1") from which human consciousness can truly evolve toward Spiritual Consciousness ("The Promised Land"). The Holy Promise is threefold ("3"): a new Land (consciousness), a spiritual Seed (Truth) and the potential as a Blessing to all nations (Commission). The immediate journey to the new land is short, but the Land of Spiritual Promise turns out to be completely undeveloped; yet, when recognized, it is a befitting birth site where spiritual potential can be brought forth, nourished and cultivated. Soon, however, with a drought of true spiritual awareness, the Hebrews again abandon their newly-endowed habitation for bondage in Egypt; to them, the Land of Darkness. They are not nearly ready for Passage into this stage of their Spiritual Path.

With Abraham's (then Abram) return to the Promised Land, after his slaughter of the kings who had captured Lot, we are given the first powerful symbol of Transformational Rebirth in the account of Abraham's encounter with Melchizedek. Although rarely mentioned, Melchizedek is perhaps the most important mystical figure in the Bible except Jesus, Himself. In fact, it was even said of Jesus that "Thou art a priest for ever after the order of Melchizedek" (Hebrews 5:6). Melchizedek was both King of Salem and a Priest of God Most High. His only appearance in the Bible is to give Abram a mysterious blessing and anointment in a ceremony of Bread and Wine. Melchizedek's connection with Christ and the obvious symbols of Inner Communion and outer commitment represent the Prototypical Rebirth from the human to the Spiritual. With the blessing of Melchizedek, the Spiritual Nature became ruler of both the intellect (King) and the emotions (Priest). It represents the emergence and synthesis of a new level of Being, later symbolized in the name-change from Abram to Abraham (Genesis 17:5). Abram was transformed from a militant to a Spiritual Warrior and from a tribal chieftain to Father Abraham, the Founder of three major Religions.

The most immediate result of this transformation, through a ''miracle birth,'' was that a promised son (awareness of our **"Only Begotten"** True Nature) was born to Abraham and Sarah (formerly Sarai). The story then ends by poignantly reinforcing the divine reality and spiritual validity of our **Sonship** (Inherent Christhood) as our **Real Identity** with the touching incident of the mistaken and uncalled-for ''sacrifice'' of the **"First Born."** This classic allegory of seeming miraculous Birth and Rebirth represents the Inborn Divine Potential and Spiritual Possibilities constantly available to each of us in the process of our transformational soul growth and development.

Abraham's son, Isaac, a child of the Covenant, mostly represents a passive phase for processing the New Awareness and consolidating the gains of the inaugural, rather discombobulating lessons involved in first setting out as Spiritual Pathfinders. Isaac's son, Jacob (enticed by his father's immature portrayal of ''nonresistance'') again attempts a deceptive shortcut to his spiritual heritage. This roguery resulted in his expulsion from home and a remedial return to the original land of his ancestors. Here he learned to patiently and laboriously work out the requirements of the law necessary for a reentry into his original homeland with a name-changing higher awareness. In contrast to Jacob's early human struggles involved in the abortive attempts to supplant the worldly birthright of his firstborn twin, Esau, was his initiatory spiritual bolstering by the remarkable visions of the Ladder of Ascending and Descending Angels. This represented a new contact with God and the assurance of spiritual ministration on all levels of living. Then, consummately, in wrestling with the Angel ''of his Higher Nature,'' he was blessed with a Transpersonal Birthing into a higher state of dominion - within himself - and reborn ''Israel'' (''Prince of God'').

Abraham's greatgrandson Joseph, with his ''coat of many colors'' (creative imagination), represents the increase in character of our limited five-sense consciousness raised into a position of great worldly stewardship by gallantly applying higher ideals of truth to adverse circumstances and emerging spiritually victorious. He used his influence to rescue his family and tribe from another drought in the Promised Land and bring them again to Egypt, seemingly a fortunate retrieval from a human point of view.

But here the Hebrew people repeated a descent into a 400 year period (a symbol) of intolerable bondage to lower, human consciousness. Then Moses ("to draw from water," or Divine Consciousness), the Lawgiver - under the authority of the I AM - introduced the knowledge of the law-governed outer control of human conduct and its hidden inner Science of Thought and Feeling and becomes the Liberator for the next major level of human advancement. It was no small task to lead the Israelites out of their enslavement. Moses was the only one who had received the necessary inspiration. The rest were still not ready for the life of Spirit, and every step of the way in the wilderness had to be proved out over and over. It took stiff discipline and firm determination to exert any kind of control and there was much resistance and many lapses and back-slips. Gradually, the older generation was replaced by a new breed of youth, a very important example of thesis-antithesis-synthesis activity. They were trained up as warriors.

When at last they were ready and the long delayed crossing into the Promised Land was at hand, the stalwart Moses was denied access! Just once he had taken too much credit for something God had actually done. This astonishing turn of the story is meant solely to demonstrate the importance of knowing the limitations of our human intelligence and mortal efforts in the Crossover from sense-bound awareness into the Promised Land of Spiritual Consciousness. The Law is an indispensable agent in preparing our minds and hearts for the spiritual transformation of Rebirth, but even when fully incorporated into the Science of our Thoughts and Feelings, it cannot take us past the limits of our "natural man" phase of Being.

The evolving saga of the spiritual quest of the Hebrews continues when Moses' successor, Joshua, is commissioned to lead a united Israel in the actual crossover of the river Jordan and conquest of the land of Canaan. Joshua's **name** in itself, symbolized the most important Truth conveyed in this highly idealized account of the third ("3") great Israelite attempt at entering the Promised Land. The name Joshua and Jesus have identical meaning in the Hebrew language: "Savior." They both originated from a word that meant **"I AM that I AM."** The abiding promise of the "Burning Bush" is repeated through Joshua: "As I was with Moses, so I will be with thee"

(Joshua 3:7).

The Predicaments and the Prophets

It is sombrous to relate, but the Hebrews (deriving from the Semitic root "to cross over") never fully occupied the "Promised Land." Many struggles are described in the following accounts found in the Bible. First, there is a period of militant regimentation and aggression. Subsequently, there emerged a reverse swing into autonomic chaos with the occasional emergence of local "Saviors" ("Judges") in emergencies: a very premature venture into "Theocracy," the Government of God by immediate Divine Guidance through heroic individuals. The Book of Judges does provide a far more historically accurate depiction of the complicated and lengthy settlement of Canaan than the Patton-type "Holy War" approach of the Book of Joshua.

The pendulum swung again toward intense worldly ambition, dreams of empire and the consequential collapse of this national aspiration within the Rise and Fall of the Monarchy. Next came a civil war that divided the Nation in two, followed by two captivities, the destruction of the Temple in Jerusalem - and another chance to return, rebuild the Temple and launch a brand new start.

Within all these caprices and misfortunes, the Hebrew Seers and Prophets (in dire terms) warned the Hebrew people and encouraged them to return to the Ways of the Covenant. The Proverbs mainly represented the "Natural man's" wisdom. The Psalms more often conveyed the inspired insights and experiences of the "Spiritual man."

Isaiah delivers his ecumenical vision in three ("3") discernible categories of literary and inspirational gradations. In the first (Chapters 1-39), he reiterates the past transgressions of the Law and then foretells of the coming Messiah ("For unto us a child is born, unto us a son is given: and the government shall be upon his shoulder..." Isaiah 9:6). He points ahead with a legacy of our "hope of glory" for the future: Emmanuel, "God is with us." In the second category (Chapters 42-55) he dispenses a vision of redemption ("The voice of him that crieth in the wilderness, Prepare ye the way of the Lord, make straight in the desert a highway for our God'' Isaiah 40:3) in which he discerns the Highest Truth of God's True Nature and adopts a universal view of Gods' Kingdom: The infinite, universal absoluteness of God's goodness and love and the beauty and glory of God's Indwelling Presence (''But they that wait upon the Lord shall renew their strength; they shall mount up WITH THE WINGS OF EAGLES; they shall run, and not be weary; and they shall walk, and not faint'' Isaiah 40:31). It had been his prophecy that Yahweh's people would return and rebuild Jerusalem and the Temple. He then anticipated the marvelous spiritual influence they could become for the rest of the world if they began to cultivate Higher Consciousness within themselves:

> ''Enlarge the place of thy tent, and let them stretch
> forth the curtains of thy habitations; spare not:
> lengthen thy cords, and strengthen thy stakes. For thou
> shall spread abroad on thy right hand and on the left;
> and thy seed shall possess the nations, and make the
> desolate cities to be inhabited'' (Isaiah 54:2,3).

He concluded by reasserting the emphatic need to recognize our human limits and allow God's Spirit to be the Senior Partner in our consciousness:

> ''For my thoughts are not your thoughts, neither are
> your ways my ways, saith the Lord. For as the heavens
> are higher than the earth, so are my ways higher than
> your ways, and my thoughts than your thoughts'' (Isaiah
> 55:8,9).

''Third Isaiah'' (Chapters 56-66) portrays the climactic vision of ''A new Heaven and a new earth'' (Isaiah 65:17): The Great Synthesis of a spiritually regenerated Life for all humankind. It also restates the Commission for the children of Israel to serve the great work for which they were chosen. They are to be seeds of reconciliation and Lights for a new spiritual world order, with ''peace like a river'' (Isaiah 66:12). Old states of infirmity and infamy will be devoured with the ''Fire'' and ''Sword'' of Spirit. ''They that sanctify themselves, and purify themselves behind one tree in the midst (''the knowledge of good and evil'') shall be consumed together'' Isaiah 66:17. Jerusalem will ''rejoice'' in the purification and transformation of all consciousness from the ''Natural man'' to the ''Spiritual man.'' Nothing from the old, lower consciousness will afflict them again.

Ezekiel, in his strange, apocalyptical imagery and mystical symbology, presents both an encouraging and reproving vision to the Jews at a crucial time of dispirited crisis in their thinking. He lived and wrote with the captives in Babylon. This exile had been the "straw that broke the camel's back" for their faith in "The God of Israel." They felt that they had completely lost contact and were forever alienated from their God. Ezekiel's task was to convince them that, no matter what had happened to the Temple and their beloved Jerusalem, Yahweh was still with His people even in their exile. How did Ezekiel know? He had experienced his own intimate, personal, experience of the Divine Presence Indwelling in this foreign land. They could do the same! Ezekiel is especially hard on the past transgressions of the Hebrews as well as their enemies, with dreadful warnings to their oppressors. But the promises are also elaborate. It is a matter of individual choice. The responsibility is theirs for the way things would go from there.

His visions are rich in esoteric symbology. There is, in Chapter One, the inaugural vision of the "four faces of man" with "four wings" ("the likeness of four living creatures"); symbolizing the ("4") formative aspects of our unfolding nature ("man" - physical, "ox" - emotional, "lion" - mental and "eagle" - spiritual). Then follows the chariot vision of a "wheel" (and "a wheel in the middle of a wheel") that turns, yet ever continues in the straight way. This is the Divine Promise that no matter what turn of events may occur, when centered in God, the crooked places will be made straight, our spiritual path will advance true and undeviating - **the eagle will soar**. There is further assurance of inward guidance and spiritual deliverance out of all our worldly distresses and encumbrances, "And the sound of the Cherubims' wings was heard even in the outer court, as the voice of the Almighty when he speaketh" - "the Cherubims lifted up their wings to mount up from the earth" (Ezekiel 10:5,16). There is also the parable of responsibility concerning the **Royal Eagles** (Chapter 17), "Great eagles with great wings," that carry the seeds of the King's tree, with roots "planted in good soil by great waters," to the highest mountain where they will grow and bear fruit.

Ezekiel's vision concluded with a repatriated Israel, not

as a nation, but an ideal state of existence in a new spiritual consciousness. With the numerical symbology of the ''Sacred
Cubit,'' Ezekiel delineates all the ways that the Glory of God
(fundamentally as an Indwelling Presence - our ''hope of glory'')
will fill the Temple (us). ''And the name of the city from that
day shall be, the Lord is there'' (Ezekiel 48:35).

Other Prophets progressively helped raise the common
human conception of God. The long process of driving out fear
began with Amos' idea that God is just. Hosea also introduces
the seed idea that God was merciful and loving. Micah brought
the idea of social justice and the ever so relevant promise, ''And
they shall beat their swords into plowshares and their spears
into pruning hooks'' (Micah 4:3). Jeremiah taught the responsibility of individuals for the control and mastery of their own
lives.

Elijah and Elisha were a study in generational polarity.
Elijah is best remembered as the ominous, unpitying ''firebrand'' emissary of doom and gloom who single-handedly took
on the entire political-religious system, including the infamous
Jezebel. Yet, he was the very one that eventually made the
illustrious 180 degree conversion to inward spiritual sensitivity
with the discovery in a ''Cave'' (inner experience) that God is
found not in the wind, nor in the earthquake, not in the fire, but
in ''a still small voice'' (I kings 19:12). Elisha, his more
sophisticated successor who wanted a ''double portion,'' the
''first son'' heritage, of his teacher's power, was chiefly a
miracle and wonder-worker. His main contribution was again
through outwardly-oriented humanistic social action and the
leadership of an urban religious group.

Joel's prophecy is typically an exhortation for repentance for the approaching Day of Yahweh. His prophecy also
contains a promise (''new wine'') of both new consciousness
and material blessings after the deliverance:
''And ye shall know that I am in the midst of Israel, and
that I am the Lord thy God and none else: and my people
shall never be ashamed'' (Joel 2:27) - ''And I will
restore to you the years that the locust hath eaten''
(Joel 2:25).
With repeated references to the Temple, there is hope expressed
for a glorious future for Jerusalem, Judah and perhaps the Jews

of the Dispersion. Yet there is also a seed of universalism:
"And it shall come to pass afterward, that I will pour out my
spirit upon all flesh" (Joel 2:28) - "Ye are the temple of God"
(I Corinthians 3:16).

The Psalmist often elevated the image of God from
representations based on fear and foreboding toward that of a
Loving Presence. With the captivity came the idea of a Universal God of all humankind. Generally, from the Prophets, we
learned to believe in One Omnipresent God, understand our part
of a Divine Partnership and to contact God by the inner way of
law and prayer.

It was from an obscure and generally overlooked Minor
Prophet, Habakkuk, that we are given a mystical insight of
unusual importance in correcting our inadequate concepts of
the Ways of God. His prophecy can be of unique value in raising
our belief in God's Goodness into a new understanding of the
mysteries of Divine Providence. Little is known about Habakkuk
outside the Book that bears his name, other than that he was a
cultish, philosophical Prophet. He received the oracle in a
temple just before the first Judean captivity and applied it
generically to all people of all times. He raised the question of
theodicy, "the defense of God's goodness and omnipotence in
the view of the existence of evil."

The literary form used in the Book of Habakkuk contains
a fascinating replica of an ancient "High Watch" communion
technique. This formula involved looking down as though from
a watchtower on historical events in the making; then "up-
wardly" asking God questions (prayer) and listening for
the answers (meditation). In the face of the captivity of the
Judeans, for example, Habakkuk addressed the issue of "un-
punished" evil and wrongdoing within the context of the one
famous statement in the Book, "Thou art of purer eyes than to
behold evil, and canst not look on iniquity" (Habakkuk 1:13).
It was a question - and a complaint: "Why are you indiffer-
ent?", "Why don't You look down here Yourself and see
what's going on?". Then the light came, a higher vision of the
Divine Plan. Habakkuk stated it as a ruling principle for all
humanity: "Behold, his (the evildoer's) soul is lifted ("puffed")
up, it is not upright in him; but the righteous shall live by his
faith" (Habakkuk 2:4). In God's Great Plan of Good, all

inflated human-ego-based negation of the Creative Process carries the seed of its own eventual dissolution. All righteousness lives on through its own inner, spiritually-based integrity. This revelation is the Divine Promise that, in time, all evil is doomed to be overthrown by the triumphal activity of God's Goodness from within through living in the light of the consciousness of the Divine Presence. The final answer to Habakkuk's question is found in the meaning of his name, "Embracing God in prayer."

Classic Bible Stories

Many modern issues are found in ancient stories of the Bible. The Song of Solomon (Song of Songs), for example presents the first evidence of feminine liberation in the Bible. This personalized application of the Polarity Principle regarding the role of male and female is one of the most important concepts that has been missing in humanity's strictly patriarchal attempts at human development and spiritual advancement.

The Books of Ruth and Jonah, in unforgettable narrative, presents the corrective principle inherent in our perfectibility of learning by our mistakes. These books are also piercing protests against racial and religious prejudice; they contain a true and heartfelt understanding of the privilege of being "Chosen People" as the commission to share God's Gifts with all people and not keeping any good thing to one's selves. The Book of Esther gives the other side of the coin: that, although the universal, loving God is equally concerned with all humanity, there is also unfailing care for the "Chosen People." The message is, no matter how bad things get, keep trusting and holding on!

The Book of Job, the "Charlie Brown" of the Bible, gives an extraordinary insight into the universal human experience of affliction and the age-old question of why the righteous suffer. Job is "perfect and upright, and one that feared God and eschewed evil" (Job 1:1). The story begins with a scene in heaven involving God and Satan and a wager about the true condition of Job's character. At that time Satan was considered part of the Divine Staff, a servant of God as a "Testing Agent" - somewhat like a bank examiner. (The legend of Satan fighting God and being sent out of Heaven originated just before the

Birth of Jesus. The notion of God's Judgement against gam-
bling developed somewhere else along the line.) This "Celestial" bet results in Job's suddenly finding himself crushed and
overwhelmed by calamity. He then asks one of humanity's
oldest questions: **Why?** This brings the onslaught of his three
"friends," categorically similar to the approach of many professional religionists, philosophers and scientists. With much
debate, they accuse and lecture Job about all the deliberate and
unconscious "sins" that he so virtuously pretends not to have
("...who needs enemies"). They maintain that he is simply
paying off his long accumulating and well-deserved debt to the
Law of Cause and Effect. To them, the only cause for suffering
is evil. God then reproves Job's friends for condemning him
and having no remedial answer.

The conclusive turning point in this classic story is when
God enters the drama and directs Job's attention to the transcendent majesty of the power, order and greatness of God's
Creation in contrast to the smallness of what Job can accomplish
or even conceive of. Job is awed into silence. God has a
magnificent Plan and we are limited in our human vision and
understanding of everything that concerns the spiritual attainment of the Divine Purpose in our lives. It is especially when
we feel "perfect and upright" in our human attainments that we
often need to be "dragged kicking and screaming" into our next
level of Highest Good. The transition from the limited mortal
self and personal rightness into the Spiritual Self and true
righteousness of Christ is never based on formal sanctimonious-
ness (which is the basis of much religious self-righteousness -
much condemned by Jesus). We are never Born Again through
any masterminding, pious exertion or ritualist observance on
the human level. That, at best, is preparatory only.

Ultimately, God reveals a different answer to "Why do
the righteous suffer?" They don't! Suffering is often involved
in growth and evolution. It is part of change, often as our
deliberate and unconscious resistance to it. This is essentially
a message for spiritually awakening people. Our growth is a
Creative Process. Trust the Process! Part of the Paradox is
that sometimes what appears a disaster is the very means of our
awakening to Spiritual Life. Pain always signals a message.
And it is often through our problems that we make the greatest
gains. Problems provide a strong incentive for improvement.

They can force us to withdraw our reliance upon outer things and to discover and rely on our inner resources. And in the long run, crisis is more instructive than destructive.

Earth is our collective classroom. Its purpose is not to make our life easier or indulge us like spoiled children, but to teach us to use our experiences to develop into stronger, mature, more creative beings. It is not easy to be a learning, growing, creative human being. Most often we learn by overcoming obstacles. Like children, we fall many times. The important task is to avoid living so cautiously and passively that we never fall. We should endeavor to live committed to the full, and always pick ourselves right back up. Nor are we ever here just to ''audit'' life's courses. Everything we encounter can teach us something we need to learn. Yet, if we had our human way, we would often try to miss all of this and, therefore, most of our growth opportunities. (Imagine having to master mathematics without ''problems,'' or foolishly praying to have them eliminated from the curriculum!)

Trust in the working out of God's Plan for the Supreme Good in your life - in spite of everything! Let go of personal concepts and be open to a Higher Vision and a new, Spiritual Perspective. Remember, when Job humbled himself to God's Omnipotence he ended up with twice as much. Even more wondrously paradoxical, the Entrance to this Higher Life seemed to open to him precisely when he got out of his attachment to himself and prayed for his friends.

Between the Testaments

There is a hiatus in the written history between the Hebrew and Christian Bible. But much occurred in this period of biblical silence. When the Jews returned to Jerusalem and rebuilt the Temple, they revived the Spirit of the Covenant. By this stage in its history, the Hebrew Nation had been led through all the disciplines of the mystical Kabbalah tradition for Transformation in a wide range of worldly experiences. These included a trained and active intelligence, a reign on human-ego pride, the cleansing and purification of the subconscious, the resolution of inner conflicts and the reconciliation of inner drives and motives by balancing intellectual disciplines with spiritual exercises - thus establishing God as their Partner and then serving as an Agent for God in the rest of the (Gentile) world. But these experiences were scarcely understood by the average Jew, and most of them, as well as the Nation as a whole, were not as yet responsibly capable of personally practicing these mystical "Tree of life" energy-flow systems for spiritualizing their own lives.

This interval between the Old and New Testament represented another dark period in Jewish history. When they were allowed to return to their Promised Land from captivity, they found themselves surrounded by foreign influences. For protection, Ezra reestablished strict law enforcement for every conceivable phase of living in order to isolate the Jews from this contamination. Then the Jews found themselves subjected to the dominion of two more world empires, first the Greek and then the Roman. After many outrages, they mounted a very courageous revolt under the leadership of the dynasty of the Maccabees. Among the Jewish groups that organized to fight for the Law (Torah) were the Pharisees. Eventually, as their original purpose was completed, they began to dedicate themselves to another challenge concerning the Law - this time within their own religion.

Obeying the law had gradually become a formality; the Hebrew people not only began to lose sight of the spirit of the law but waned in their compliance. The Pharisees readopted Ezra's reformation and committed themselves to a renewed puritanism and the separation of Jewish life from everyone and everything that was ritually unclean. They implemented the Jewish rules of conduct into their chief means of worship and salvation. In this position as stewards of the Law, the Pharisees became a powerful society of religious men among their own people.

Concurrently, an aristocratic priesthood also emerged into prominence within Judaism. They were known as the Sadducees and were tenaciously conservative in their political tendencies - particularly in appeasing and placating their Roman conquerors. These two opposing organizations of the learned Pharisees and the privileged priestly nobility of the Sadducees, comprising the Sanhedrin, ruled the Jewish Nation with ritualistic and sacerdotal autocracy. They shared one commitment: maintaining the status quo.

The Birth and Life of Jesus

It was into this background that Jesus was born. Another man was born into the same setting at almost the same time, John the Baptist, one of the most colorful figures in biblical history. He provides the clearest representation in the Bible for the important distinction between the "Natural man" and the "Spiritual Man" and the most explicit statement in Scripture about the Great Paradox involved in Spiritual Transformation.

The contrast between John and Jesus is fascinating. John begins his ministry first. He is the forerunner of Jesus, an Elijah-like and charismatic preacher of repentance, endorsed by Jesus as the necessary initiation form of preparation for the Higher Life of Spirit: "The voice of one crying in the wilderness, Prepare ye the way of the Lord, make his path straight" (Matthew 3:3). He was an outstanding example of the traditional, primal point of view of wanting to live righteously out of fear of a wrathful, avenging Jehovah and for the special rewards invoked by repentance and reform. John's method typically was first to warn and scare people into changing their ways and then to promise the imminent appearance of "the Lord's Anointed."

John's real mission was to help people prepare to change their minds. He baptized in water, symbolizing a mental cleansing, a letting-go process of washing away old, limited concepts. This purification rite represented the first step leading to the Baptism of the Holy Spirit: the opening of our consciousness to the quickening of the Christ Spirit and a transformation of mind and heart in the realization of Spiritual Truth. John attracted a great deal of attention. He had come out of the wilderness with harsh raiment (severe personality) and his food was locust (bitter denunciation): "O generation of vipers, who hath warned you to flee from the wrath to come" (Luke 3:7). His fame spread rapidly and it soon reached the ears of the Jewish leaders that his message included loud political protest. He was arrested for troublemaking and breaching the peace and he was eventually beheaded.

Jesus acknowledged John as an exceptional person, but lacking a vital dimension:
"Verily, I say unto you, Among them that are born of women there is none greater than John the Baptist:

notwithstanding he that is least in the kingdom of heaven
is greater than he. And from the days of John
the Baptist until now the kingdom of heaven
suffereth violence, and the violent take it by
force'' (Matthew 11:11,12).

John, of course, represents the ''Natural man'' - the
highest and best that can be done with our human resources and
intellectual development. Even more, John is an outstanding
example of a high intellectual recognition of Spiritual Truth -
the transitional stage just before the great mystical breakthrough, when fear and all its desolating and disruptive guises
of separation will be replaced by a consciousness of peace, love,
awe, respect and unifying Oneness. It is especially John's
struggle with evil as a reality that demonstrates how the reasoning of the intellect, no matter how highly developed, can go only
so far. The main function of the intellect in the Spiritual Process is to pave the way for Enlightenment. Trying to storm
heaven with intellectual and emotional violence culminates in
imprisonment (the soul-constriction involved in fighting what is
perceived of as evil). This leads to eventual death (the necessary demise of the ''head'' rule of the human-ego- personality
level of life). John recognizes this. ''I baptize with water: but
there standeth one among you, whom ye know not; He it is, who
coming after me is preferred before me, whose shoe's latchet I
am not worth to unloose'' (John 1:26,27). ''He must increase,
but I must decrease. He that cometh from above is above all:
he that is of the earth is earthly, and speaketh of the earth: he
that cometh from heaven is above all'' (John 3:30,31).

Jesus believed, above all, in a God of love, a beneficent
Parent Spirit of infinite goodness. His whole Life was the
embodiment of a perfect expression of God's All- Good Nature
in a human life. John recognized the difference and was
reverently in awe of Jesus. What is remarkable, however, is that
John himself never followed Jesus. He kept right on in the old
way. The John the Baptist movement actually rivaled Christianity for several hundred years. Its influence still permeates
much of modern Christianity. This shows the great tenacity of
the human-ego identity in persisting in the path of the ''Natural
man,'' with ''No room in the inn'' of the intellect for the Birth
of the ''Spiritual man.''

Jesus, nevertheless, began where John had established his work. He was baptized by John, a sign of letting go of His former activities and taking up His Divine Mission and His New Way and signifying that the highest way to begin all things is in the inner birthing of a spiritual commitment. He also chose six of His Disciples from the work of John. The theme of Rebirth into Spiritual Living continues throughout Jesus Ministry. Even in His Own Birth, the role of Herod, the Wise Men, the Shepherds, Joseph, Mary, as well as the Inn, the Stable and the Star in the East had revealed deep mystical insights into the inner activities of our minds and hearts in the Birth of the awareness of the Indwelling Christ Child in our own consciousness.

We know very little about Jesus' actual childhood from the Gospel, except that He assigned immense value to childhood itself in the spiritual process of Rebirth and Transformation: "Except ye be converted, and become as little children, ye shall not enter the kingdom of heaven. Whosoever therefore shall humble himself as this little child, the same is greatest in the kingdom of heaven" (Matthew 18:3,4). In such regenerating contrast to the debilitating Doctrine of "Original Sin" (never mentioned in the Bible) Jesus sanctioned the validating and empowering concept of "Original Innocence" - the humble, meek, guileless, trusting, teachable, optimistic and lovable receptivity to Spiritual Truth.

One of Jesus' strongest warnings was against contaminating this childlike consciousness with the falseness of negativity: "And whosoever shall offend one of these little ones that believe in me, it is better for him that a millstone were hanged about his neck, and he were cast into the sea" (Mark 9:42). The spiritual symbology of this last scriptural reference reveals quite a different process and more positive outcome than a literal translation - the encouraging promise conveyed in the word "better" is the key. When spiritually discerned, we find that everything Jesus said and did illustrated some aspect of the creative process involved in Spiritual Rebirth and the ongoing possibilities of our Spiritual Transformation.

It is in the **Last Week** of His human life that Jesus devotes His teachings exclusively to the Crossover into Spiritual Identity and the Entrance to the Spiritual Consciousness.

The **Triumphal Entry** (based on the Old Testament Prophesy "Rejoice...behold, thy King cometh...lowly, and riding on an ass.." Zechariah 9:9) demonstrated the way the Messiah enters into our consciousness, not on "a great white horse" of human aggrandizement but in the Spiritual Triumph of humble and joyous acceptance of the Way of Spirit.

The **Footwashing** again, emphasizes the importance of the spiritual purification of our "understanding."

The **Betrayal** gives an unforgettable precaution about the notorious tendency of our zealous intellectual perception to "sell out" to the ways of the world and perhaps attempt to force the Spirit into conforming to a limited human vision.

The **Lord's Supper** presented as the central Mystical Experience in celebrating the Christ Life, is a beautiful tradition for Inner Spiritual Communion in the mystical "Marriage" of the human and the Divine with the appropriation of The Bread of Spiritual Truth and the Wine of Spiritual Consciousness into our entire Being.

The **Upper Room Teachings** like the Sermon On The Mount, is a compact gold mine of Jesus' Spiritual Discourses in which Jesus connects His **(I AM)** Nature with ours and extends the vision of life into its Eternal Context ("many mansions") - the total human submission to the Divine Will.

At the **Trial** Jesus was completely in charge of Himself and beyond defending Himself, the ultimate expression of nonresistance and one of the highest achievements of a human life.

The **Cross**, which Jesus glorified, is one of humanity's oldest symbols. It represents each and every human being - and the convergence of his or her Divinity into their humanity. Paul and the early Christians did not focus on the Cross as an emblem of our sin and shame, but on Its promise of Resurrection - the synthesis-point of spiritual upliftment between our (horizontal) human discipline and God's (vertical) Transforming Power into a new, Larger Life: "I (Christ Indwelling), if I be lifted up from the earth, will draw all men (human ego-personalities) unto me" (John 12:32) ("As above - so below").

With Jesus' **Crucifixion** "The veil of the temple was rent in twain from the top to the bottom; and the earth did quake, and the rocks rent" (Matthew 27:51): His Ultimate Unveiling of the long hidden Spiritual Truth of our Being ("Know ye not that **ye** are the **temple** of God, and that the spirit of God dwelleth in you?" (I Corinthians 3:16); dislodging every worldly-based untruth with an open demonstration of God's Power within us ("as within, so without").

Jesus' **Seven Last Words** the Cross (steps that paradoxically can be reversed) are Statements of Completion ("7") of the Creative Process disclosed in His earth-life Mission.

His **Resurrection**, the ultimate Rebirth in this life, opened the "windows of life" to the Eternal Things of Spirit; proving that we are more than physical and can be Spiritually Resurrected into a New Conscious ness every time we rise up out of the tomb of limited beliefs.

Cutting the Apron Strings

In the forty days between Resurrection and Ascension, Jesus consummated the training of His Disciples for their Apostleship, "cut the apron strings," and launched them on a Commission based on the belief in their own Indwelling Spirit. Jesus Ascended so that His Spiritual Presence also could be with everyone, "And lo, I am with you always, even unto the end of the world" Matthew 28:20) - as we can Ascend into New Consciousness and New Life by realizing (making Real) that Presence Within.

It is in the Acts of the Apostles, initiated with Pentecost and the confounding of their accustomed rational expression, that we see their Spiritual Birth into Transformed lives. The transformation started small and grew gradually. They had missed much of the Spiritual Context of His Teachings and, at first, merely waited for Jesus to return physically. They especially missed the connection of their Apostolic Commission as being Lights in the world. The pointed example of Jesus' immediate return to His own work in the valley after the Mount of Transfiguration was lost on them, and they completely missed the mark in wanting to be disassociated with the world and evacuated from earth-life. Again we have the paradox in which this physical life often appears in conflict with our Spiritual Destiny.

Earth is an educational experience for the soul, but not our only teacher. We are earth-bound and trapped in a world of physical senses only in our perception. Jesus turned us over to another Teacher from Within, the Spirit of Truth that "will guide you into all truth" (John 16:13). We can dwell in the Higher Realms ("not of this world"), link our Nature to the Universal, pass from the temporal to the Eternal, and still gain the benefits of all the lessons and opportunities while "in the world." This paradox is resolved in an integrative (holistic) approach to life: mentally, emotionally, physically and Spiritually.

The Transformation from lower to more advanced states of consciousness pivots around a change in our self identity, the ego-focus of who and what we think we are ("...Whosoever will lose his life for my sake"). John the Baptist had identified himself with the "Natural man," human nature, and dwelled in that illusion. Jesus would have us identify with the "Spiritual man," Christ Nature, and dwell in that Truth ("deny himself, take up his cross and follow me"). To be Born Again is to awaken to the Truth of our **Original Birth** as God's Spiritual **Image and Likeness** ("Who is the image of the invisible God, the **firstborn** of every creature" Colossians 1:15), we are to claim that Birthright and begin to bring our Divinity into our humanity ("**I AM** one that beareth witness of myself").

Rebirth is the realization of our forgotten Spiritual Nature and the Birth of that Nature into our human nature. We take on the Ego of the Christ ("I and my Father are one"). It is a miracle of change from self ("Son of man") to Self ("Son of God"). It does not eliminate our human nature, It Transmutes it ("unless a corn of wheat die..."). It moves us into a higher state of consciousness that manifests our Spiritual Potential into our human possibilities and transcends our human limitations ("Why callest thou me good?"). The "Spiritual man" is born out of the "Natural man" and our humanity becomes more! We live an entirely New Life from a Higher Power ("The Son can do nothing of himself") and learn to recognize our earth experience and humanity as marvelous Gifts ("Treasures upon earth") for our spiritual education and Soul advancement ("Treasures in heaven").

The Mystery of Revelation

Many years after the Ascension of Jesus, The Apostle John, through a spiritually matured vision, reiterated in the masterful Book of Revelation all these metaphysical insights of spiritual transformation and inner evolution into the Higher Life of Spirit. He revealed this as a process that takes place in us. For protection against the Roman Persecution and for the spiritual discernment of those "who have eyes to see," Revelation was codified in Kabbalistic-like symbology. The number "7" (applied 55 times to visions, churches, seals, candlesticks, trumpets, stars, angels, bowls, plagues, etc.) carries the theme of the Divine Fulfillment involved in specific stages of progressive spiritual development and consummation in the world of phenomena. This is based on the pattern of the Seven Steps in Genesis I. Much of the bizarre Eastern symbology concerns the importance of understanding the need in the **synthesis** process for cleansing and reconciliation within the human unconscious (the "habitat of dragons"). It also involves understanding the propensity for our often ferocious, internal psychological "civil war." There is striking imagery representing the inner conflict that can occur between our old (parent) human beliefs and new **thesis** Spiritual Perceptions ("I bring a sword...and come to set a man at variance against his father...") as well as the externalized **antithesis** resistance ("Armageddon").

An important symbolic number in approaching the frontier of the Paradox is the number **"6"** (Hexad), **the symbol of man** and the highest step of exclusively human attainment possible in the Seven Steps of the Creative Process of manifestation. The villainous **"666,"** the "mark of the beast on the forehead," unforgettably marks the limits of the human intellect in bringing forth the spiritual blessings of our "Sixth Day"

Divine Image Heritage. The tradition goes back to the Great Pyramid and the Initiation Passage from the Ascending Gallery into the King's Chamber and the Holy of Holies. In between the two is an Antechamber in which the walls symbolically change from limestone (Human) to granite (Divine), with three "lows" causing one to bow three ("3") times before entering ("Every knee shall bow" Isaiah 45:23 - the "Natural man" to the "Spiritual man"). The diagonal dimensions of the floor ("cross") contain the "666" symbolic representation of leaving behind the limits of the intellect for the wisdom of Spiritual perception: "Here is wisdom. Let him that hath understanding count the number of the beast: for it is the number of a man, and his number is Six hundred threescore and six" (Revelation 13:18).

No matter how we multiply and compound (or computerize) it, human intelligence alone cannot visualize and direct the attainments that will lift humanity into the higher state of Creative Living that awaits our Spiritual Rebirth. Intellectual acumen can't even attempt to solve the present global problems of war, hunger and environmental havoc that it originally created without soon letting the mark of greed, glory, aggrandizement, self-interest and self-promotional success as the world knows it show on the "forehead" (personality). The "bottom-line" self-concern-above-all-else way that our governments, industries and religions respond to the responsibilities they represent is often "beastly." When we take an Archetypical Idea from the Universe and attempt to use it in human life, we have to know what we are doing. The intellect, without the added inspiration and power of Spirit (the Seventh Step) is never capable of spiritual fulfillment.

The Great Pyramid's "sacred" geometric proportions and symbolic measurements of the King's Chamber ("Holy of Holies"), Sarcophagus (ritualistic tomb of Resurrection) and the missing Capstone ("The stone which the builders rejected" Matthew 21:42) - symbols of Christed Consciousness - are later translated into the Biblical Ark of the Covenant, the Temple and the "New Jerusalem."

But this cryptic message of "Christ in you" has never been imparted to the "masses." It is this in particular, the individual attainment of spiritual understanding through direct, personal Divine Revelation (their real contention with Gnosticism - while assimilating much of the Gnostic negative dualistic tradition), that has been the biggest threat to the authority of the historical "Priesthood" in their self-appointed intercessory role. The perpetuation of ecclesiastical sovereignty has been the ulterior motive behind all the inquisitions, condemnation and attempted eradication or invalidation of rival spiritual disciplines. The religious hierarchy kept this for themselves. But, then again, this spiritual dispensation has never been much questioned or even desired by the average "Natural man," whose goal in life has fallen far short of the "mark for the prize of the high calling of God in Christ Jesus" (Philippians 3:14), which is accomplished by letting "this mind be in you that was in Christ Jesus" (Philippians 2:5).

The quest of the human intellect is rarely for true wisdom; rather, it is for the worldly security of "certainty" (control). The intellect can display much genius with endlessly clever and manipulative devices in horizontally dispersing the opportunity for change into neutralizing, ineffectual and constraining systems and institutions. The demand for certainty and the desire for control is the motivation and justification for dogma and doctrine.

With all its mental aptitude and polish, this strategy for conformity and dominion can correspond only to the worldly-constrained, unenlightened level of the "intellectualized" sparrow: the domain of Lucifer, "The Prince of the Intellect." Whereas, it is the characteristic symbolized by the **eagle** to seek ever farther beyond the horizon of knowledge and rise with the elation of Prometheus to meet the spiritual challenge of the unknown:

"Beloved, now are we the sons of God, and it doth not yet appear what we shall be: but we know that, when he shall appear, we shall be like him, for we shall see him as he is" (I John 3:2).

The Province of our Intellect

As with our humanity, though, we are not to scorn or depreciate our intellect. We are to recognize and utilize its right(eous) function. Spirit requires a good intellect and a strong, healthy ego as working partners. Our human mind is the flight path to the Infinite Mind of God. Much of the Disciple-ship of Jesus is precisely about training our minds and building a consciousness aligned to Spiritual Truth that allows Spirit to elevate our minds and work through our uplifted lives.

Our intellect has a very important role in our lives. There is much for which it is responsible in our spiritual growth and development. It is in charge of the discipline, direction and quality control of our thoughts. It initiates inner corrections and reconciliations of the conflicting and competing issues of our heart. It inaugurates resolutions for the unfulfilled parts of our being and calls forth all our faculties and powers and guides and coordinates them in right and balanced use. The intellect accepts and sanctions our whole being as spirit, mind and body and relates everything in our lives to this holistic perspective. It can reach past our present limits and allow vertical gains in our consciousness, pushing up the boundaries of our minds and hearts by going even beyond positive thinking and altering our view of life with the birthing of as yet unthought thoughts and undreamed dreams. Our intellect is also the agency through which we author our prayers and by which we can invoke divine help in continually surpassing our former selves, mentally, emotionally and physically.

Like Moses (Law), our intellect is instrumental in taking us to the Border of the Promised Land. It sets the foundation for Higher Life by cultivating a consciousness of the qualities, values and ideals of the "Spiritual Man." Maintaining the right supporting concepts in our day to day thinking is vitally impor-tant to our spiritual interests. We aren't likely to fly with the **eagles** if we roost with the turkeys. It is the constant obligation of our intellect to be willing to leave former concepts behind, move out of the prevailing lower common denominator and go beyond the range of habitual thoughts that have been attached to the human ego personality and focussed on the material. It has much responsibility in the human arena of everyday life, but the goal must always be subservient to Spirit and all the earthly enterprises of Spirit ("the Father's business"). It must invite the inspiration and soul nourishment of Communion and initiate spiritual growth, but not apprise or direct it.

This final step is the number "7" (Heptad), the **Sabbath**, in which we retreat inwardly, rest, touch the Creative

Silence, "Wait on the Lord" (Psalms 27:14); and, in this "not of this world" consciousness, completely let go and let God be God in us. The key is receptivity, the Grail Cup open and receptive to the inflow of Spirit - and the Mystical Union of the human and the Divine.

Mark Twain wrote, "Life does not consist mainly or even largely of facts and happenings." The Second Bondage for the human mind is the dependence upon cerebral intelligence ("6") for the Spiritual Awareness that lies beyond the limits of fact and reason - the Mystical ("7"). When the intellect is made the master of the mind, we are the suffering servants. This is the meaning of Jesus' intellectually paradoxical statement "Which of you by taking thought can add a cubit (Spiritual Amplitude) unto his stature?" (Matthew 6:27). As with Moses and John the Baptist, our intellect and human personality can never take us into Spiritual Consciousness. The purpose of all spiritual ("esoteric") symbology in the Bible is to point us beyond the literal boundaries and rational limits of our intellectual comprehension and help establish in us a receptive abode for Spiritualized Consciousness.

Fare Thee Well

In His Farewell Address (John 14:2) when Jesus said, "I go and prepare a place for you," He meant in our Predestined Estate of Christed Consciousness: the Mystical Place of Absolute Truth where we truly know and abide in the Spiritual Realization of our own Eternal I AM Identity, "I and my Father are one." "And if I go and prepare a place for you, I will come again, and receive you unto myself; that where **I AM**, there ye may be also." Jesus prepared a spiritual legacy of Christ Consciousness that each of us can appropriate and assimilate into our minds, hearts and lives.

Yet, even assuming to intellectually conceptualize these higher realms of Spiritual Truth in terms of the "absolute" as an attempt to attain a "place" from which we artificially divest ourselves from worldly "illusions" (not fully realized Truth) becomes an escaping into abstractions and only traps us on the other side of the Paradox. Instead of attaining "that mind in you, which was also in Christ Jesus" (Philippians 2:5), we enter into a mind-game perspective of "high-level" denial that seems

so confusingly "unreal" to our underlying human senses that it
results not only in an unbalanced and uncreative response to the
opportunities at hand, but also the soul-encumbrance of almost
inevitable self-righteousness and uncompassionate detachment.
One of my teachers once said, "As long as we are in the skin,
we are skinners." We are not to "judge" and abandon the
world with our evolving knowledge of Spiritual Truth, we are
to be receptive and allow the infinity of Truth to help transcend
our ordinary human perspective and responses. Those who
truly follow "the Way of the Christ" accept life each moment,
live it fully committed and bring Truth into every experience.

The Science of our Thought and Feeling ceases at the
Border of the Promised Land of Spiritual Consciousness. It
cannot proceed from there. Then the Great Paradox becomes
a reverse polarity. It inverts. We do not enter the Mystical,
It enters us. The "water" of our human consciousness transforms into a "new wine" of Awakened Spiritual Awareness.
The Holy Grail begins to fill. Christ Returns in us. "Every
good gift and every perfect gift is from above and cometh down
form the Father of lights" (James 1:17).

Then, through the spiritual synthesis of the creative
process in us, our two natures, human and Divine, blend into a
oneness of consummative unity (a "marriage made in heaven").
A new dimension and quality of consciousness is born within us.
We are "transformed by the renewing of our minds." (Romans
12:2) We abide more and more in a Living Stream of Creative
Consciousness charged with Life, Light, Truth and Love. We
become vibrant-ly alive with forgiveness, peace and good will.
It lifts us from the limits of unenlightenment to the new possibilities of a Transcendental Perspective.

By living in a consciousness of God's Living Presence,
"dualistic" facts and ideals merge into a New Reality. The
Truth we have intellectually and emotionally established in our
minds and hearts becomes spiritually activated. Our inner
powers and faculties become divinely reinforced. As did Jesus,
we acknowledge and honor both our humanity and our Divinity.
We behold the holiness in mundane affairs and the sacredness of
our planetary home. Through our emerging Christlikeness
(Roman 8:29,30), we become Sacred (Glorified) Humans. We
are "in the world," but "not of this world."

An Exchange of Will

As seen at Gethsemane, the sentinel at the gate to the spiritual side of life requires an exchange of the human will for the Divine Will. The human will, the faculty of immediate determination at the control-point of our intellect ("6"), has been given the formidable ability (like a spiritual warrior) to take a stand against all the prevailing wrong influences of the rest of the mind and heart and redirect the entire consciousness toward a new estate of living ("4").

It is also through our will that we can consciously and devoutly offer up, on the Altar of Spiritual Truth, the Grail Cup of our inner lives (as a spiritual womb), sacrificed ("Made Sacred") and emptied of all that is humanly less for the Rebirth of all that is Spiritually Greater ("7"). There is an ancient saying, perhaps the final resolution of the Great Paradox in the crossover from the "Natural man" to the "Spiritual man," that "The will can have anything that it does **not** desire."

The Last Barrier

The last barrier on the Frontier to the Promised Land of Spiritual Life is materialism. This is poignantly dramatized in the haunting story of the Rich Young Man who asked Jesus "What lack I yet?" (Matthew 19:20), but sorrowfully could not bring himself to exchange his "great possessions" for "treasures in heaven" - and follow the Christ. Alas, "No man can serve two masters" (Matthew 6:24).

Through the will, the vested interest of the human-ego must surrender its own attachment to materiality. The encumbrance is not the use of an abundant supply of material things for supporting the legitimate needs of this life and providing us the necessary physical frame and fabric for learning and growing. It is the often very subtle ("serpentine") ego-possessive, materially-oriented life itself. If we learn to appreciate the manifest world of the five senses ("5") in its proper sustaining relationship to God's Plan for our Highest Good, we will know that energy, matter, form, appearance, time and space are divinely gifted allocations for our benefit. With right use, they are great allies in our spiritual advancement. Our foremost obligation for all this is to remember to put "first things first."

The paradox of the "rich man and the camel" can be resolved in the knowledge that the "needle's eye"was the name of a gate in a wall of the old Jerusalem that, for defensive reasons, was so small that a camel could only enter if the commercial load was first removed from its back. The material supply for our earth-lives is not meant to burden and bind us as the finite object and priority of our existence. Our goals must always extend beyond the loaves and fishes towards liberation from the material, to the point that we are willing to "pluck out our right eye" (envy) and "cut off our right hand" (greed) - unmasking and repudiating the **real** "Satan," human egocentrism in all of its pretentious guises.

As the **eagle** rises up from the earth, it soon loses interest in the repiles, toads and mice. When the Old Adam (primitive persona) "dies" and the Snake (radical egotism) "gives up the ghost," the "Second Man" (Twice-Born - with a complementary New Eve) ascends into the full spiritual service of the Lord and enters a Heavenly Partnership with God (see I Corninthians 15:22, 45-49).

The Sword of Truth

The life of a Spiritual Apostle is a sword-blade's edge of balance between the needs of the physical and the priorities of God's Will, always guided by the Divine Polestar of the human will, "But seek ye first the Kingdom of God, and his righteousness; and all these things shall be added unto you" (Matthew 6:33). It is most resulutely established and maintained within a Covenant of Stewardship. With this process, our own life inverts. We undergo the paradoxical metamorphosis from "Know Thyself" to the equally important "Forget Thyself" - and we live for something bigger than ourselves. By rising out of our lesser selves and serving others, we really discover what Jesus meant when He talked about "losing your life" to gain Larger Life and promised that "The first shall be last and last first."

We also come to know that it truly is more "blessed to give than to receive." We choose to live with the verb "to be" rather than "to have" and abide in a **consciousness** that possesses "all things that the Father hath" (John 16:15). "I am the Alpha and Omega, the beginning and the end. I will give unto him that is athirst of the **fountain** of the **water of life** freely. He that overcometh shall inherit all things; and I will be his God, and he shall be my **son**" (a full-fledged partaker of God's **Only Begotten** Divine Nature - see II Peter 1:4) Revelation 21:6,7.

Once the crossover has been initiated, the important remaining discipline is in maintaining a "Yin and Yang" polarity balance between the passive inner joy of spiritual consciousness and the thrill of outward creative action in a synchronized flow of Oneness ("My Father worketh hitherto, and I work" John 5:17). This balanced state of expressing spiritual qualities from the Inherent **Characteristics** of our own Inborn (and Reborn) Christ **Nature** in our human nature is the criterion of all true success, happiness and enduring fulfillment ("And they shall see his **face;** and his name shall be in their **foreheads**" Revelation 22:4). "Blessed are they..."!

A Marriage Made In Heaven

In the Bible, Jerusalem often symbolically represents the history of the consciousness of humanity. The "New Jerusalem" is the spiritualization of human consciousness. "And I John saw the holy city, coming down from God out of heaven, prepared as a bride adorned for her husband" (Revelation 21:2 - first introduced in "Third" Isaiah 62).

The Beautiful symbology of the "Mystical Marriage" ("2") between the human and the Divine is the requisite of all Rebirth and Spiritual Transformation ("3"). The consummation of this Spiritual Union inaugurates the epochal advancement into a new Era of Spiritualized living: The confluence of the "Alpha and the Omega" (perfect spiritual wholeness) into the here and now; "As above, so below"; "As within, so without"; "In earth as it is in heaven" ("7") - "But in the days of the voice of the **seventh** angel, the **mystery of God** ("which is Christ in you, the hope and glory" Colossians 1:27) should be finished' (Revelation 10:7). When this occurs in our own personal lives, we become party to a miracle: Spiritual Reality and human fact unite and become One in a Divine Unity of Purpose.

The Sermon of the Mount closes with the picture of two houses caught in a cloudburst. One is built on rock, the other on sand. The consciousness of Spiritual Truth is upheld by the Eight ("8") (Ogdoad) Step process. This symbolic number represents a durable support for a **cyclic new spiritual order** and regeneration level of the soul. It also points beyond the completion of the "7" to "A new heaven and a new earth" (and "New Man") of Jesus' eight Beautiful Attitudes. It will stand up under any challenge earth-life might hold in our Divinely Assigned "tour of duty" here and initiate us into even higher (I AM) potential for living in the **spiritual life** from **spiritual consciousness** ("Blessed our they that do his commandments, that they may have right to the **tree of life,** and may enter in through the gates into the city **(New Jerusalem)**" Revelation 22:14).

No matter what the current "in the world" situations, conditions, and circumstances are, the opportunity for higher awareness and spiritual expansion is always "at hand." The present moment is always right for inviting the "not of this world" divinely infallible influence for God's Higher Good into our minds and hearts and lives. "Ask, and it shall be given you; seek, and ye shall find; knock and it shall be opened unto you. For every one that asketh receiveth; and he that seeketh findeth; and him that knocketh it shall be open" (Matthew 7:7, 8).

Paul, an Apostle by the Will of God

It was the Apostle Paul who perhaps best realized and gave expression to the resolution of the Great Paradox. As we have seen, he had been born with almost everything the "Natural man" ever wants, works for and even prays for. Then, on the road to Damascus, came the spiritual vision of the Living Christ and his quantum catapult into spiritually awakened consciousness. It didn't even make his life easier.

First, like Job, everything he had possessed in a worldly way was taken away. And certainly his new perspective of the world was not always through "rose-colored glasses." Nor did the transformation immediately convert his personality into all "sweetness and light," or instantly bring forth full mature expression of his Divine Potential. Many of his letters expressed a theology widely recognized as different from that of Jesus. His letters were sometimes shrouded in negativity and often laced with criticism, dispute, controversy, dissension and grave disappointment in others; for which among other things, he more than once landed in prison. He was hard on himself, too. "For that which I do I allow not: for what I would, that do I not; but what I hate, that do I" (Romans 7:15).

Twice, near the beginning of his new life, he had withdrawn into complete abandonment from the world. He went into seclusion, possibly to lick some ego-personality wounds, probably to assimilate his "uninvited" spiritual experience and undoubtedly to gradually nurture and prepare himself for the heretical and heroic new destiny that awaited him. All which is to say that Paul, not withstanding the extraordinary Spiritual Dimension to his life, remained very human - a man of "flesh and blood."

But Paul (originally Saul) had awakened to his Reality of his Divinity as the Sacred Compliment to the corporeality of his humanity, bridge the Great Paradox and crossed the Spiritual Frontier into the Land of Promise. In Jesus words, he "put his hand to the plow," did not look back - grew in Spirit and Truth - and became "fit for the Kingdom of God" (Luke 9:62) with ultimately one of the optimum spiritually successful lives in history. Paul, himself, summed this up with six of the most creative words that can be incarnated into the Capstone Fulfillment of a Self-Realized human life in the Mystical Process of Spiritual Transformation: **"For me to live is Christ"** (Philippians 1:21).

Chapter Thirteen

The Great Commission

"And He said unto them, go ye into all the world and preach the gospel to every creature" (Mark 16:15). These words spoken by Jesus to the Disciples, whom He had trained for three years to carry on His Precepts and Example and then ordained as Apostles, came to be accepted as The Great Commission of the Church. From this charge, through an organizational Apostolic Succession, Christianity became an evangelical ("One who proclaims the good tidings") religion, true to some extent of all the major religions of the world. In many ways the spread of Jesus' Gospel has been successful. Much of Western Civilization is now Christian, although a large segment of the world still adheres to other religions.

Over the centuries, Christian Churches of every denomination have provided sanctuaries of worship, retreat, solace, hope, encouragement, faith, cheer, ceremony, peace, beauty, fellowship, festivity, teaching, inspiration, charity and even havens of safety for their congregations and communities. There have subsequently been many, many good Christians who did their best to live their lives based on the religious and individually inspired understanding of the Gospel of Jesus Christ and to minister to others in "His Name" (His Consciousness and Example).

Counter to this, sometimes incongruently, the overall organized institutional strategy for world conversion has not always conformed to these Teachings or presented itself anywhere near to the Example of Jesus; the Divine Model of peace, compassion, forgiveness and brotherly love. Most of the doctrines and dogmas of Christianity were developed to facilitate the proselytization and control of converts. The "good tidings" (an ecclesiastically acquired Salvation and the Parousia - Arrival - of Christ) came to be couched so often as such bad news, chiefly an arousal of primeval fear within the threat of the "End of the World," Eternal Punishment and a despotic "them and us" predisposition toward all Non-Christians.

It was for this very freedom from domineering and abusive religious practices - and the indispensable mandate of separation of church and state - that constituted one of the main reasons the United States of America was founded. There is little need to further elaborate on the grievous history of intrusive narrow-mindedness, rigid moralism, cruel and sometimes violent atrocities, bloodbaths and genocide inflicted on countless individuals, entire cultures and nations through the misunderstanding and misrepresentation of Jesus' Gospel.

In studying the history of the Church, not infrequently one is jostled into a recollection of Jesus' repeated exhortations about hypocrisy, as well as Emerson's more recent rejoiner, "What you are shouts in my ear so loud that I can't hear what you are saying." The aggregate consequence of the adjunct to Jesus' Gospel of evangelistic propagation on the world at large has been somewhat like having a cow that gives a generous supply of milk - and then sticks its foot in the bucket.

Emissaries of Light

In order to rightfully understand the amazing possibilities of our actualized spiritual influence and then the responsibility carry out The Great Commission - and therein, also avoid all harmful repercussions - we must penetrate the spiritual significance and intention behind Jesus' Initiation of Spiritual Apostles charged with representing Him as Emissaries of Light into the world. We need to clearly discern what He, Himself, said and exemplified regarding all facets of this Christ-Appointed Mission.

First, it is important to grasp the real meaning of what Jesus was imparting to the floundering Disciples (and, therefore, all of His eventual Followers) just before His departure:
> "But because I have said these things unto you, sorrow
> hath filled your heart. Nevertheless, it is expedient
> that I go away; for if I go no away, the Comforter will
> not come unto you; but if I go, I will send him to you"
> (John 16:6,7).

He would not allow even the Radiance of His Divine Example blind us to the discovery of our own latent Divine Potential; and in turning us over to the Comforter, He removed the Brilliant Attraction of His own Physical Personage as a possible deterrent to embracing the "Hope of Glory" possibilities (Colossians 1:27) of our own spiritual growth and development. He then spoke of sin, judgement and righteousness, and opened the way for the resolution of all these - right within ourselves - by the Advent of an Innate Spiritual Countenance and Power. This came to be known as the Holy Spirit, first manifested to them both personally and collectively on the Day of Pentecost.

It can clarify a great deal to understand that the "Holy Spirit," with all of Its history of definitions and special designations, essentially means "The Christ Spirit in the Present Tense." Jesus couldn't have been more pointed in telling us that His return would transcend the limits of an external physical appearance: It would be Spiritual. The truth is, He isn't "coming," He never left!

In the "final interview and commission," during His appearance to the Disciples after His Resurrection - as the Risen Christ - when Jesus promised "Lo, I am with you always, even unto the end of the world" (Matthew 28:20), He was again rending the veil of human understanding and disclosing the essential inwardness and spiritual constitution behind the Gospel Universal. The only possibility that He could have been referring to with this all-embracing promise would be the personal Spiritual Realization of a Divine Presence and Power; something that can be testified to by countless individuals, from the Apostle Paul on the road to Damascus right into the present time, including this author.

Jesus came to bring the Spiritual Truth to all humanity. Everything concerning His Message, His life and His Example to us can be understood only from a spiritual perspective. We have stood earth-bound looking to the sky and missed Jesus' entire spiritual meaning about Heaven, Hell, Salvation, Damnation, the "Coming," the "End of the world," Eternal Life and, every bit as important, the Presence of a Latent Christ within each of us - attested to by Paul's words of extraordinary spiritual acumen and worth engraving into every human heart: "The mystery hid for ages...which is Christ in you, the hope of glory" Colossians 1:26,27).

Paul's Spiritual Interpretation

In fact, let us look at Paul's interpretation concerning our Spiritual Commission:

> "Do we begin again to commend ourselves? or need we, as some others, epistles of commendation to you, or letters of commendation from you. Ye are our epistle written in our hearts, known and read of all men: foreasmuch as ye are manifestly declared to be the epistle of Christ ministered by us, written not with ink, but with the Spirit of the living God; not in tables of stone, but in fleshy tables of the hearts. And such trust have we through Christ to God-ward: Not that we are sufficient of ourselves to think any thing as of ourselves; but our sufficiency is of God; Who also hath made us able ministers of the new testament; not of the letter, but of the spirit; for the letter killeth, but the spirit giveth life" (II Corinthians 3:2-6).

Paul had been continually challenged by the Jerusalem Apostles as a self-appointed, counterfeit Apostle because he had not known Jesus "in the flesh" (Perhaps the real "thorn" in his flesh). As a result, Paul often defended his Spiritual Apostleship, especially in his frequent introduction of himself in his Epistles as being "Called" by God through the Christ Spirit. From his original life-changing encounter with the Living Christ, Paul knew that the indwelling Christ Spirit (which he equated with the Holy Spirit) was, in contrast to anything legalistic or worldly, the only true authority for anything concerning the interpretation of the Spirit of the Gospel or anything else divinely communicated. He dismissed all the rest as "false teachings."

The first of many religious controversies in the spread of Jesus' Gospel began almost immediately. At the center of the long-running dispute between the Jerusalem Apostles and the Apostle Paul was the disagreement over who should be converted and how it should be done. The Apostles in Jerusalem linked everything to Judaism, insisting on adapting Jesus' new ideas into strict conformity within the observance of traditional Mosaic Law and being a good Jew as first importance (the ceremonial issue at that time was circumcision and not how water should be applied for Baptism). Paul insisted even more indefatigably on letting the barriers down and sharing the Gospel with all Gentiles. The Jerusalem Apostles waited in

Jerusalem for Jesus' Return.

It was the Apostle Paul who ventured out into the world on missionary journeys, preaching, teaching and often improvising and justifying that which was locally expedient for the conversion of not only practicing Jews, but Hellenistic-Greek and Roman-imperialistic mentalities wherever he found them. It was Paul's own special interest in converting the Roman Empire to Christianity that set the pattern for the eventual ecclesiastical church organizations that evolved in the Western World. Sometimes to Paul's consternation, he opened Jesus' life and teachings to a much broader, increasingly Westernized, philosophical and religious interpretation than orthodox Judaism - while losing almost all touch with the underlying knowledge and spiritual understanding of the Hebrew's deep, well-protected mystical tradition (Which Paul openly addressed as **"The Mystery"**: Romans 11:25, 16:25,26; I Corinthians 2:7-16, 4:1, 15:51-56; Ephesians 1:9-14, 3:1-9, 6:19; Colossians 1:26-28, 2:2,3, 4:3,4).

Above all, as a Jew, Paul had come to recognize the restrictive limits of exclusiveness that had gradually evolved in the prevailing Jewish Messianic hope for deliverance from their worldly enemies and a restoration of God's promises to them as the "Chosen People." Paul then realized that by the time Jesus was born, He didn't fit their accrued overlays of religious qualifications and expectations for the "Anointed One" (Messiah). It was this Gospel of spiritual recension, the revealed Mystery of the all-inclusive, **Christ-in-every-child-of-God** Messianic "Hope of Glory" (Colossians 1:26,27) that Paul established as first importance in his own transcendent strategy of evangelism.

The Missing Mystery of the Messiah

With two thousand years of further doctrinal overlays, however, the true universal spiritual mission of Jesus still doesn't fit the qualifications and expectations (and restrictions of exclusiveness) of most people now. Nor has the **Mystery**, and its Spiritual Perception of Reality, yet penetrated the hard shell of Western literalism. Instead, bit by bit, the concept of Salvation has changed. Ultimately, Salvation encompasses the all-embracing blessings of Spiritual Wholeness: Christ's "Ran som'' of reinstated **At-One-Ment** for all our ''missed marks,'' gracious delivery from our human mistakes and spiritual enlargement of our soul. But the meaning has been doctrinally reduced to a personal physical rescue operation based on the profession of certain dogmas and creeds, rituals and membership in specific denominational religions. The current sectarian term of exclusion, ''Rapture,'' was originally symbolic of the mental and emotional exaltation of Spiritual Transformation. The alteration from the glory of a transcendent inward spiritual experience into an instantaneous bodily evacuation of the religious ''elect'' into Heaven (much used in ''bumpersticker'' evangelism: ''Warning - the driver may suddenly disappear from this car'') was invented in England a little over a hundred years ago. As Joseph Campbell once exclaimed about all these pitifully hidebound notions: ''For Heaven's Sake!''.

The Biblical references cited in this ''End of the world'' scenario is the strictly literal translation of apocryphal (codified) symbols associated with the Appearance. This includes key metaphysical words and phrases such as the following:

> **''Tribulation''**: from a word referring to a threshing floor, the important process of separating the wheat from the chaff preliminary to our human ego deferring to the Rulership of Spiritual Consciousness - the Kingdom of God within;

> **''Coming in a cloud with power and glory''**: symbolizing the veil of mystery through which Christic Consciousness triumphantly enters human consciousness;

> **''In the twinkling of an eye''**: the Transformational Process instantaneously invoked when, ''In the fullness of time,'' our human consciousness is ready to be introduced to a higher vision of the Truth of our Being; and Spiritual Illumination can forthwith cut through all the hard-shelled defensive resistance, ignorance, pain, fear-based beliefs and their multiple layers of illusion with the glorious Revelation of the Spiritual Heritage awaiting us as Children of God growing up into our latent Christhood.

Truth Sets us Free and Makes us New

We have probably never realized how much the contemporary evangelical concept of Salvation is limited to fear-based, negatively motivated incitement. Nor have we recognized the egocentric appeal and pious pride behind our conversion and religious practices; often relegating our Great Commission almost exclusively to recruiting others into the ecclesiastic restrictiveness of our own "only 'only' religions."

One of humanity's great deliverances will come with the redeemed understanding of "Judgement"; not as a terrifying time of condemnation, doom and the everlasting punishment of an angry God's "fallen creatures" (a strictly eschatological fear-tactic closely fettered to an ancient Hebrew conception of the Day of Yahweh and the punitive practices of the "Judges" of Israel) but judgement "That all men should honor the Son, even as they honor the Father" (John 5:23): The reinstating and recommendatory bestowal of new spiritual insight, valuation and understanding of the True Standard of our Being in a Born Again awareness of the Father's Image in us. Judgement serves as an interlude of Divine Appraisal and Spiritual Accounting, a **"face to face"** imparting for the highest and best with release from the mistakes of the past ("missed marks"), the consolidation of our spiritual gains and a grace-filled New Start in Christ. "Judgement Day" can be **every day** a time of Enlightenment and Spiritual Breakthrough: "A white stone, and upon the stone a new name written" (Revelations 2:17).

The word "Salvation" ("Return to the Source") is closely linked to the word "wholeness" (as well as "peace"). The crux of Jesus' Gospel can be understood within His summons of Spiritual Transformation, "Be thou made whole": Be redeemed and restored to your original Divine Heritage from within yourself ("Be ye therefore perfect..."). In the Gospel of Thomas, the apocryphal writings of the Life and Teachings of Jesus, He is quoted as saying "Bring forth that (which is) within yourself, that (which) you have will save you." Salvation, inaugurated through the grace of an inner liberation (peace) and a higher realization in consciousness, is a holistic (Holy) new integration of our total nature and a leap forward in the progressive order of the Pathway of our Spiritual Development. We are Saved essentially from our own ignorance and illusions ("And ye shall know the truth, and the truth shall make you free" John 8:32).

Paul likewise linked Christ's Return to a much higher consideration as a New Creation: an establishment of a New Spiritual (peace filled) Age to come under a New Covenant of the Spirit with the termination of an age passing ("The end of the world"). In the Bible, the words "world" and "earth" are sometimes used interchangeably. But there can be a meaningful differentiation. God created the Earth, our beautiful planetary home and provided everything needed to sustain us here in a worldly paradise. We all share the one Earth, both in its potential bounty and in its misuse. On the other hand, by giving us the power to "name things" (Genesis 2:19), God has allowed each of us to create our own world - which is our perception, at any time, of how things are. It is the old world ("Our own little world") of illusory perception that will end with the advent of the Spiritual Perception of Christ Consciousness. The original Greek "Aion" did not mean "The end of the world," but, in Paul's perspective, "the end of an age," or "cycle."

The Way Christ Appears

The theme of the return of Christ developed soon after the Ascension, when the Disciples expected an immediate reappearance of Jesus. Although He did not physically return as they had anticipated, the phrases "Second Coming" became part of Christian eschatology in 150 A.D., giving a literal interpretation to a mystical idea.

The Second Coming can occur in our personal world anytime we invite the Spiritual Influence of the Christ ("Holy") Spirit to enter our minds and hearts and receive the power from "On High" to express the Christ Nature (Messianic Consciousness) in our own lives. It will come to pass "world-wide" as the cumulative consciousness of illumined individuals attain a "critical mass" perspective of Spiritual Oneness and create the One spiritually unified World in which we all may contribute and share the blessings of Christ Consciousness ("Glory to God in the highest, and on earth peace, good will toward all" Luke 2:14). The consummation of Christ's manifold Return is when Christ lives through all of us.

Most of the years of Jesus' life have been omitted from the Bible, like a huge piece cut out of a cake with a knife, as though it weren't considered important for us to know anything about them. But I have found it inspiring and fascinating to contemplate what surely is one of the greatest Unknown Events in history. There had to have been a time in Jesus' youth - a supreme Moment of Truth in His life - when He discovered His own Messiahship and was Anointed with Messianic Consciousness; and, perhaps, recognized the enormous challenge involved in His Great Commission to reveal Its true quintessence to an unenlightened humanity.

We know from the only glimpse we have into his early life at the age of twelve, in a dialogue with the Temple Scholars, that He possessed an exceedingly precocious understanding of the Jewish teachings and their Messianic Expectations. Perhaps one day in study or prayer, Young Jesus may have suddenly realized: "WHY, I AM THE MESSIAH!" "Not I alone am, in my `Son of man' human incarnate identity, but **I AM** - my identity with the `Son of God' Christ Spirit indwelling me, as well as that of every one else, the same I AM that delivered the Jewish Nation from bondage through Moses - is the **Messiah**." This is the Principle revealed within His amazing (and grammatically perplexing) statement, ''Before Abraham was, I AM'' (John 8:58).

The great Salvation Message is that the Christ Spirit can live in each one of us - personally. And, if we open our consciousness to Its transforming influence, This Indwelling Lord-Of-Our-Own-Being becomes an everpresent, all-powerful Source of constant help. It also becomes a minute-by-minute Salvation from every ''fallen'' belief, fear, illusion, care or need we shall ever face in this life - whether it be a cut finger or small irritation, or the most serious ailment, predicament or calamity possible in the world - from anything that holds us in bondage and prevents us from expressing that which we were created to be as Spiritual Beings.

This fuller view of Salvation, whose other name is Truth, places our allegiance where it needs to be: God-In-Us, our very present help in every need. Jesus (accepted as a ''Personal Savior'') is the great Example of the Christ life, the life that is possible for every Child Of God. Following Him lifts us from our personal (''Adam'') self, to which we eventually shall all ''die''; and then be reborn into the Spiritual Sonship for which we were created "In God's Image."

The High Vision

    Jesus said "In my Father's house are many mansions" (John 14:2). With the vastly expanded view of the universe from the advent of the New Physics, nearly every schoolchild knows that most of the universe exists outside of our human concepts of time and space. Eternal Life does not mean endless duration of time; it is a quality of life expressing the fullness of God Within in the present moment: God's Spiritual Time - the "Eternal Now." Likewise, "damnation", (which has come to be linked with "Eternal") from the human standpoint actually means no more than "blame" - the consequential spiritual blockage and soul stagnation resulting from our childishly trying to duck our own responsibility for correcting and expanding our lives by shifting the blame outside ourselves (starting again with Adam, and the primordial "cop-out": "The Devil made me do it!").

    Even more significant, as shown by Jesus' repeated example of condemning only the "sin" and never the "sinner," from God's standpoint, it is only negative states of consciousness and their effects that are "damned" (blocked out), never people (Souls). This confirmation of God's everlasting grace, divine release and spiritual renewal is unforgettably accentuated in Jesus' classic parable of the Prodigal Son's no-strings-attached, open-armed, loving reception from the Father. As Paul indicated in his introduction to the aforementioned chapter concerning the Old Ministry and the New, "Are we beginning again to commend ourselves?", we limit our own progression in spiritual understanding by our human ego-pride and worldly vested interests in the religious beliefs and establishments from the past.

    This is how Paul concludes his third chapter of II Corinthians, in which he identifies the qualities and glory of our Spiritual Apostleship as ministers of a New Covenant and a New Era In The Spirit when the veil is "Done away in Christ": "But we all, with open face beholding as in a glass the glory of the Lord, are changed into the same image from glory to glory, even as from the Spirit of the Lord" (II Corinthians 3:18). Jesus came to reveal "The Truth and the Life" - found in Christ

Consciousness and entered into by being "Born Again" - into our original and everlasting true Spiritual Identity.

The Messiah - as is the Kingdom of God, Heaven, Salvation, Rebirth, the Second Coming and all aspects of the spiritual Gospel of Jesus Christ - is, in essence, within. They all emanate from the Spirit of God (Christ) that dwells within every person. When we express God in our lives, Christ has appeared in us. We, from within ourselves, are the "epistle," the Living Gospel of God's Spirit that abides in each of us. The only mark of a true Christian is how much Christ shines through! Everything else "misses the mark." This is a very important distinction. Jesus, most definitely, established a positive "Solar" religion - based on the Divine Radiance from the Son Within: "The true Light, which lighteth every man that cometh into the world" John 1:9). All too often, this has been negated into the soul-repressing, primal "Mars-like" tactic of bellicose recruiting, inciting and controlling converts - predicated on providing alarm and fear of a menacing adversary with the incessant need for continuously inventing additional externalized "enemies" to demonize, repudiate and assail.

Accordingly, as we approach Jesus' criterion for representing Him "Into all the world," it is imperative to understand that the method and character of the "means" are indispensably linked to the "ends." Jesus, Himself, represents God in all the magnificence, splendor and majesty of a spiritually perfect and essentially flawless Creation - the "Word made flesh" of a beautiful Creative Process in which mistakes serve only to bring about higher Good and only the Good endures in an ever-unfolding, upward, onward procession "Christ to God-ward." And, in taking up our own Great Commission, we, too, become the "Word made flesh," Ambassadors in our world for God. And, we too, like God, are to so love the world that we bring forth our "only begotten" Spiritual Nature: "Glory to God in the highest"! Therefore, rudimental to Spiritual Apostleship is an awe-filled reverence for the "Eternal" dignity of the Office Of The Christ Indwelling; a respect that prevents our zealous personal will from inattentively ever devaluating the Handiwork of God's Creation, especially by demeaning the God Image in every person, crucifying the Truth about our Spiritual Potential or giving anyone cause to be misled or embarrassed for Jesus for any unseemly way that we might misrepresent Him.

Two Memorable Metaphors

In the Sermon on the Mount, Jesus used two simple, but memorable metaphors, "Salt and Light," to convey the Christlike attributes, characteristics and creative influence of His Spiritual Apostles. "Ye are the salt of the earth" (Matthew 5:13) and "Ye are the light of the world" (Matthew 5:14) are like two sides of one coin about our amazing influence when we are centered in the Christ Way of Living. If we will reach past the "letter" of these words, we will find in them an ingenious "epistle" to our hearts teaching us the Truth about ourselves and the potential of our contagious influence in pursuing our Great Commission. Simply identify and adopt their message as a personal revelation about you; and, especially, apply it within.

The Salt of the Earth

We usually become "The salt of the earth" before we become "The light of the world." "Salt" may have conveyed a different meaning in those days than it does today. Now, salt is a very commonplace and rather insignificant commodity. This undervaluation, however, might lend itself to an important starting realization. The Disciples, themselves, rather fit this subordinating classification. They were mostly uneducated, relatively poor, unimpressive, provincial peasants. As Jesus spoke, from their point of view in their world of Roman military and political might and Hebrew religious-priesthood control, they probably wondered "What can I do?" (Identify yet?). This inadequate valuation can also serve to announce that a Spiritual Appointment is not the special prerogative of those with educational, religious, political or social prominence. In choosing His Disciples from common, undistinguished individuals, Jesus was affirming the essential worth and potential value of every Child of God.

In the Bible Lands of Jesus, however, salt was actually a very valuable possession, a treasure so rare that a major enterprise was the transport of salt hundreds of miles by camel caravan. In Palestine, salt was regarded as basic to all the essential needs of life. It was most indispensable as a preservative. In fact, salt was said to have been as precious in that barren land as a person's life itself. It was a constant life-saver: no food, no life! Salt was also used for medication and hygiene.

It was the only antiseptic they knew. They used it for healing wounds, toothaches, poisons; they even rubbed newborn babies in salt for general health protection and well-being. Salt, then and now, is a great seasoning. A single "pinch" can enhance the flavor of huge quantities of food. "Salt" has been defined as "the stuff that spoils potatoes when you leave it out." "Salt" also means humor, which gives zest to living. It was also a token of friendship, the "greeting card" of those days.

Yet, salt was elevated above any undervalued status not only by virtue of its monetary value as a medium of exchange in the marketplace, but even more because of the religious eminence it was accorded as a Sacrificial Offering - a means of worship and dedication to God. So, when Jesus told His followers that they were the "Salt of the earth," they knew that He meant something really important. Part of the secret that this symbol reveals is divulged through the knowledge that life has its roots in the invisible. Many of the beneficial commendatory contributions of salt emerge in synthesis combination with water, in which salt dissolves and disseminates its properties equally to every particle, actually transforming and adding new characteristics to each molecule.

We have seen that, starting with the Genesis Creation Story, "water" is often used in the Bible as a symbol for consciousness. A "pinch" of Spiritual Truth, appropriated in any of Its specific functions such as peace, understanding, forgiveness or love, can regenerate our entire consciousness ("Till the whole was leavened" Matthew 13:33), in just the way that salt can interpenetrate and eventually saturate water with new qualities. The creative influences of those that begin to cultivate a spiritually-based life are like salt, because they begin as the silent, hidden, inner transformational forces that preserve, heal and restore those values and attributes which atone ("to make at one") and saturate our inner world with righteousness and wholesomeness. The inner work in our minds and hearts is the discipleship, "Truth-student" stage of preparation that commissions a consciousness "salted" with Spiritual Truth. Most of the basic formative work in our individual spiritual growth is accomplished as "Salt of the earth." The unseen, permeating effects of study, prayer and the application of Spiritual Principles and Laws to the ordinary things in our everyday lives transforms the "within" that becomes the "without."

As a youth, I remember the barbershop calendar pictures based on a caricature of a "Country Philosopher," a funny looking fellow in an odd hat, ill-fitting clothes, a flower in his lapel and a homely but fascinating face. It was a seasoned, weather-beaten face, but gentle with crinkling eyes and a little grin that seemed to say it all. I had the feeling that no matter how rough things might get, nothing could ever quite knock that smile off his face. It spoke to me of wit, courage, endurance: the "right stuff" of the pioneer's spirit that meets the challenges of this world in the quiet heroism of "The salt of the earth."

As we allow the leaven of our Disciple Influence to move beyond the perimeters of our own inner world and out of ourselves, we become Apostles of Truth, spreading our newly acquired higher command of spiritual worth, flavor, zest, enjoyment and other qualities of Christ to all those around us. One important quality to remember in connection with "salt" is that it loses itself (yet not the savour of its Selfhood) in what it "salts." The pragmatic proverb "It is amazing what can be accomplished when you don't care who gets the credit" could have been coined for "The salt of the earth." Salt loses its virtue only when, like Lot's wife, it crystallizes.

Contemporary Twelve Step recovery programs have proven highly successful in generating spiritual life-changes. This spiritualized power is reminiscent of the endowments and mettle of the First Century Christians before the religious quarrels inhibited and narrowed the Church into dogmatized institutionalized evangelism. Much of this power comes from the use of the Principle of Anonymity; not of hiding out, but of boldheartedly doing something good "without being caught at it" - an exemplary Christlike ministration beautifully narrated in Lloyd C. Douglas' intriguing book <u>Magnificent Obsession</u>. Only God knows the covert goodness that has been accomplished through the silent ministry of "The salt of the earth."

The Light of the World

When Jesus told us "Ye are the light of the world," it was an even more inspiring image. In those days, when the sun went down, there was no artificial outside security lighting and it became very dark and scary. Darkness represented danger,

fear and evil.   Light was the precious symbol of hope, goodness, safety, salvation and the Presence of God.   Even a little
light could make such a big difference.   What a wonderful
complement Jesus was paying to our Real Us!   He connected
us directly to God and all that God is.   "Light" is the over-all
symbol of the Divine.   Not only Goodness, Illumination and
Spiritual Transformation in expression, but the radiant activity
of Truth lived out in a Christlike Life: The Light of the Spiritual
Self.   "Ye are the Radiant Essence of Creation in action!"

   The Aramaic word for the Bible, "Auretha," means
"Light"; specifically "The Light of the mind" (the Greek
"biblia" referred to a "library"). The story of Jesus, especially, is a great drama of Light - that "True light which lighteth
every man that cometh into the world" (John 1:9).   Jesus was
the blazing light of the Christ Spirit manifest in this world.   He
said "I am the light of the world" (John 8:12).   Moreover, when
He said "Ye are the light of the world" (Matthew 5:14), He
linked our Spiritual Nature directly with His.   Modern science
has enhanced our appreciation of light even more.   We now
know that light is the one radiant energy, the creative essence
in which all things in the universe are made ($E=MC^2$). And Jesus
announced that the full spectrum of this True light is potential
in you.

   This Light is the mark of your Divinity.   Its expressions
are wide and varied, always positive, benevolent, redeeming,
and Christlike.   When Light appears, ignorance ("sin" and
"Evil") and its deficiencies vanish unto themselves.   Light
brings newness, health, joy, freedom, beauty, goodness, love
and glory.   It gives cheer, comfort and love.   Light (analogous
to the "Tree of Life" - and the Christmas Tree!) is a recurring
biblical symbol of the "Life by Spirit," in which the mysterious,
universal, infinite power of God becomes individual and personal in us.

Unity in Diversity

   The infinite diversity in which the One Spirit expresses
Itself, the heterogeneous variation in the way God distributes
talents, opportunities and challenges among humankind and the
multi-levels in which humanity perceives and experiences the
lessons that the human world can teach should make it obvious

that no one common doctrinal understanding of theology could possibly serve the spiritual requirements of all people. In addition, neither can the "Many Mansions" of Spiritual Reality ever be forced into the confines of any dogmatic belief system, or any length of religious extortion or pious imperative make Spiritual Truth conform to partisan evangelization. God is no respecter of the religious claims of particular institutions. God, Who regards each person as a unique and precious creation and relates to each as though they were God's Only Child, fulfills the universal needs of humanity from an individual basis.

God's Infinite Wisdom inspired all the different world religions in order to encompass the aggregate height and breadth of all personal growth requirements for every single Child of God involved in the collective venture of human soul evolvement. Our genuine unity, including that among all our nations, is found only in this great diversity, which brings together, balances and synthesizes all our separate and special contributions of talents, abilities and assets for our Highest mutual Good. Our authentic independence is validated in this unified interdependence: The Parenthood of God, the Brotherhood and Sisterhood of Humanity.

Reducing the Great Commission to an attempt to proselytize all others into one exclusive dogmatic mind-set pulls the Gospel down to the lowest common denominator quest for certainty and the propaganda bias of being "right," to the invalidation and defamation of all other beliefs. These doctrinal aberrations are the truly paranoiac dividing cause underneath the nationalist, economic and social justification for all human wars. The one, integrating, unitive experience common to all spiritually awakened people is the personal realization of God at work, creatively and uniquely, in their lives for the good of the whole. This is what we take into "all the world" - an individual expression of God's Light in a Transformed Life.

One of the most encouraging laws governing Spiritual Rebirth is that "Truth begets Truth." We are beginning to ascertain scientifically that humanity shares a Jungian-archetypal collective Higher Consciousness (which Emerson called the "Oversoul," Teilhard de Chardin the "Noosphere" and Rupert Sheldrake the "Morphogenic Field"). The extraordinary significance is that - when we as individuals are Trans formed - the Field of Power is increased and it becomes easier for all others to enter into Transformational Consciousness. In the process, we also tend to evolve out of self-interest into global community interests and a sense of Spiritual Oneness. Perhaps, in the metaphor of flight, we can value the contribution of the general religious doctrinal structure of the past best by considering it as a hard-shelled cocoon that has protected a beautiful butterfly while it developed enough to fly. Originally, as a caterpillar, the potential butterfly probably had no idea that it would transmute into a creature with wings. (Reputedly, one caterpillar that glimpsed a butterfly in flight said, "You will never get me up in one of those things!".) But, once a butterfly is reborn from a cocoon, it is not required to preserve or further improve the cocoon. It drys its wings in the sun - and then it is free to soar.

A Rainbow of Spiritual Light

The world is emerging from its greatest inner darkness, the ignorance of the Spiritual Truth about the Divine Nature of God vested within every human - the antithesis of "Christ in you, the hope of glory" (Colossians 1:27). Even the smallest light can kindle many other lights and guide others through great expanses of darkness.

"Ye are the light of the world. A city set on a hill (high consciousness) cannot be hid. Neither do men light a candle and put it under a bushel, but on a candlestick; and it giveth light unto all that are in the house. Let your light so shine before men, that they may see your good works, and glorify your Father which is in heaven" (Matthew 5:14-16).

We need only give the Light we have (a Truth-filled consciousness); and then trust, as Jesus did, that people can find the Way of their own Spiritual Guidance and Help from the inspiration within themselves. As Children of "The Father of lights" (James 1:17), the single life of each of us has the potential every minute to accept and express the Christ Light and extend our individual consciousness of Truth into the greater whole of humanity's total awareness - God's Rainbow of Spiritual Light. Jesus was disclosing to each of us the amazing influence for good we can be at any time as even the smallest grain of Salt or a tiniest glimmer of Light. In the days of "lamplighters" someone wrote: "I have never seen the lamplighter, but I have always known where he has been by the trail of light he leaves behind." What a wonderful way to live.

"By their Fruits"

"Wherefore by their fruits ye shall know them" (Matthew 7:20). All of humanity's true and lasting progress has been accomplished through enlightened ideas actualized through illumined minds and loving hearts. Everything created by God ultimately exists with the sole purpose of the giving of itself in loving service to the whole of Creation. Throughout history, every true hero or heroine of history was someone who gave themselves to something beyond themselves ("He that loseth his life for my sake shall find it" Matthew 10:39). Nothing of true spiritual value has ever been attained through negative concepts forced or proselytized through unenlightened thoughts, fear-centered emotions or locked-in, judgmental, self-righteous, dictatorial states of awareness. Yet, Spiritual Truth always "bears witness" to Itself - through higher human consciousness. By the very authenticity of Its Divine Nature, Truth is destined to prevail over all humanly formulated negation: the impending doom of dogma.

"**I AM** the root and the offspring of David, and the **bright** and **morning star**" (Revelation 22:16). As Children of God, our True Spiritual Nature is eternally rooted in God's Abiding Presence and foreordained to give spiritual expression to that "True Light, which lighteth every man that cometh into the world." **The Dawning Light** of our **Awakening Sonship** (God's "Only Begotten" Image and Likeness Born Again in us) cannot be hidden under a bushel of negative doctrines. "For unto us a **child** is born, unto us a **son**" is given: and the government shall be upon his shoulders: and his name shall be called Wonderful, Counsellor, The mighty God, The everlasting Father, The Prince of Peace" ("First" Isaiah 9:6). With all their vestments of authority, worldly power and intellectual stratagem, not even Pharaoh, Herod, nor eventually the entire religious hierarchy could kill the "Fresh-Born," First-Born Son.

"And a little child shall lead them" (Isaiah 11:6). With the remarkable guileless insight of a childlike heart, a little boy uttered the towering proclamation - about himself - "God don't make no junk." And, in Boys Town Founder Father Flanagan's realization, "There are no bad boys."

"And he showed me a pure river of water of life, clear as crystal, proceeding out of the throne of God and the Lamb" (Revelation 22:1). We are not flawed creatures. We are God's Beloved Children in the process of all the trials, triumphs, pains and joys involved in growing up! In Jesus' "Way, Truth and Life" of the Inner Christward Path, all our "grievous sins" are immature and unenlightened misconceptions and mistakes ("**missed marks**") to be corrected and transcended by the **Spiritual Christening** of our consciousness ("4"), not inborn "defects of wickedness" to be punished. Paul - as did Jesus, the little boy and Father Flanagan - focused on our **potential**: "I press toward the **mark** for the **prize** of the **high calling** of God in Christ Jesus" (Philippians 3:14).

Nothing has gone wrong with God's Great Divine Plan or Universal Spiritual Process for Creation. There is not a "bad" atom (or Adam) in the universe. Each has a Divine Purpose and special contribution of its own in the holistic "Big Picture" of Creation's Spiritual Oneness ("1"). Nor is life on earth a "bad trip" from which our only aspiration should be to escape or await a privileged evacuation. The great privilege is to be here ("5").

The unique earth-life opportunities for "on target" (spiritually "centered") accomplishment are enormous. The greatest growth and gain is in learning the most and gleaning the utmost good out of every situation; then giving back our very best ("6"). Jesus constantly invited us to accept our True Divine Heritage by establishing and living in a consciousness (strong inner God-Kingdom) of peace, forgiveness, wholeness, abundance, enlightenment and love; and, as Living Proclamations of the Jesus Christ Truth - with a sense of stewardship and guardian service "to every creature" - entering into and embracing the whole world with minds and hearts open to unconditional expressions of God's Nature ("7").

The goal of the entire Sermon on the Mount is to prepare each of us for the Great Commission of our life of letting Christ return where we are - as an individual expression of That Nature

- and, as resplendent, high-flying eagles, trailing ''clouds of glory'' where we have been.

EPILOGUE

It was part of my earth-life experience to fly Air Force jet fighters contemporary with the breaking of the Sound Barrier. No one had known for certain that it could be done. Even when our "speed of sound" planes inadvertently began to enter "the edge," they would shudder, and we would respectfully back off. But, with a new set to the wings and a little added power, some very skilled and courageous flyers soared on through - and, as they say, the rest is history.

Soon after that momentous breakthrough into Outer Space occurred, Spirit effected a somewhat similar life-changing entry into the inner space of my personal life. I wasn't as prepared for it as scientists were for the Space Program. Through the years that followed, I learned mainly to just "report for duty" and try my wings a little every day. I have also come to identify a good deal with the Apostle Paul. His Epistles have often spoken very nearly to what I was meeting and learning as I followed the New Path that was the inevitable way that I must go. Not infrequently the identity was "That which I would do, I do not - and the very things I don't want to do, I do." There have also been times when I shared the exalted glimpses of awareness that Paul sometimes so beautifully expressed. I have learned to discern some of the Mystery Paul wrote about. I have also learned not to kill the Mystery.

It has been a beautiful non-scriptural Poem, however, that most captured and keeps alive the inspiration of my initiative encounter with the Mystery. I first read it on the back cover of my Pilot Training Graduation book. It was written by another Fighter Pilot, just a few days before he was killed in action in the Battle Of Britain, at the age of nineteen.

"High Flight"

Oh, I have slipped the surly bonds of earth
And danced the skies on laughter-silver wings;
Sunward I've climbed and joined the tumbling mirth
Of sun-split clouds - and done a hundred things
You have not dreamed of - wheeled and soared and
      swung
High in the sunlit silence; hovering there,
I've chased the shouting wind along, and flung
My eager craft through footless halls of air.

Up, up the long, delirious burning blue
I've topped the wind-swept heights with easy grace
Where never lark, nor even eagle flew -
And, while with silent lifting mind I've trod
The high, untrespassed sanctity of Space,
Put out my hand and touched the face of God.

                  John Gillespie Magee, Jr